Common Core
Writing Handbook

Teacher's Guide

GRADE
6

HOUGHTON MIFFLIN HARCOURT

Contents

Writing Strategies

How to Use This Book

The *Common Core Writing Handbook* was designed to complement the writing instruction in your reading program as well as meet all of the Common Core State Standards for writing. It consists of two components: a handbook for students that they can refer to as a resource as well as practice writing in throughout the year, and a Teacher's Guide that supports instruction by providing minilessons for every handbook topic.

Components

Two easy-to-use components make up the *Common Core Writing Handbook* program:

- For Grades 2–6, a 160-page partially consumable student handbook with 30 writing topics that correlate to your reading program's lessons.

  The first section of each grade-level handbook includes writing models along with interactive practice to scaffold or reinforce students' under-standing of opinion, informational/explanatory, and narrative writing. As students practice writing, they build additional examples of forms to refer to throughout the year as well as develop a deeper under-standing of each form's structure.

  The second section of the handbook is a resource tool that students can refer to whenever they write. Topics range from writing strategies to how to use technology to do research.

- For Grade 1, a 96-page partially consumable student handbook also includes 30 correlated handbook topics followed by a resource section on writing strategies, such as the writing process and writing traits.

- For Grades K–6, a Teacher's Guide

with 60 minilessons for section 1 (two minilessons for each section 1 student handbook topic) plus one minilesson, as needed, for each remaining page of the resource handbook. The Kindergarten Teacher's Guide includes an abundance of copying masters.

Minilessons

Minilessons are short, focused lessons on specific topics. For each minilesson, you will demonstrate an aspect of writing before students try it. In this Teacher's Guide, minilessons are provided for each topic in the handbook. In the first section are two minilessons for each student handbook topic. Each of these minilessons consists of the following parts:

- Topic title
- Tab with section name
- Minilesson number and title
- Common Core State Standards
- Objective and guiding question
- Easy-to-follow instruction in an *I Do, We Do,* and *You Do* format
- Modeled, collaborative, and inde-pendent writing
- Conference and evaluation information

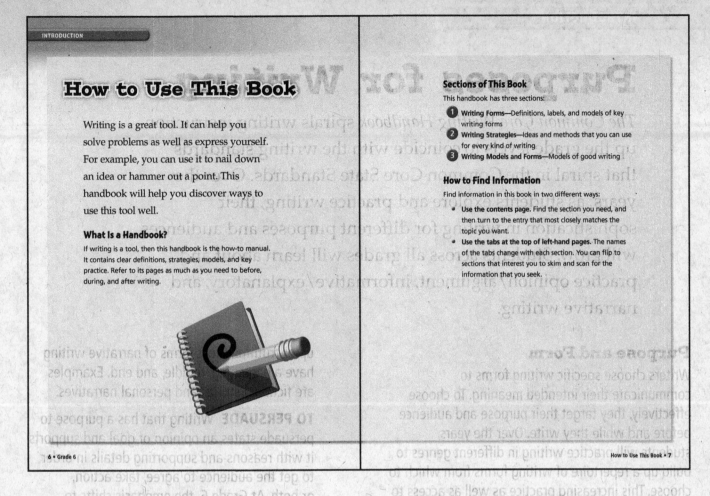

How to Use This Book

Writing is a great tool. It can help you solve problems as well as express yourself. For example, you can use it to nail down an idea or hammer out a point. This handbook will help you discover ways to use this tool well.

What Is a Handbook?

If writing is a tool, then this handbook is the how-to manual. It contains clear definitions, strategies, models, and key practice. Refer to its pages as much as you need to before, during, and after writing.

Sections of This Book

This handbook has three sections:

1. **Writing Forms**—Definitions, labels, and models of key writing forms
2. **Writing Strategies**—Ideas and methods that you can use for every kind of writing
3. **Writing Models and Forms**—Models of good writing

How to Find Information

Find information in this book in two different ways:

- **Use the contents page.** Find the section you need, and then turn to the entry that most closely matches the topic you want.
- **Use the tabs at the top of left-hand pages.** The names of the tabs change with each section. You can flip to sections that interest you to skim and scan for the information that you seek.

6 • Grade 6

How to Use This Book • 7

- Technology references
- Reduced facsimiles of student handbook pages
- Tips for corrective feedback
- A feature that further explores the lesson's writing trait

Each writing minilesson has been correlated to your reading program's writing lessons so that all mini-lessons and corresponding writing handbook pages within this section are used at least once during the school year. Additional minilessons are provided throughout the Teacher's Guide and correlate to each remaining page in the handbook. Use these minilessons, as needed, to clarify concepts for students and provide additional support.

Student-Page Walk-Through

Have students turn to and read pages 6 and 7 in their books. Explain to them that their handbook is a tool that they can use whenever they write. It can help them find information quickly about any writing question they have, and they can use it to help them during writing. Guide students to find

each of these parts in their handbooks:

- Table of contents
- Introductory pages, including over-views of the writing process and the writing traits
- Writing form pages, each with a section tab, title, definition, and helpful bulleted points, followed by a clear example of the writing model as well as a write-in activity page
- Additional reference pages on topics ranging from writing strategies to revising to using technology, as well as more examples of writing models they may need or want to refer to during the year for projects and other assignments
- An index. Remind students that the table of contents is in order of pre-sentation while the index is ordered alphabetically.

Purposes for Writing

The Common Core Writing Handbook spirals writing instruction up the grade levels to coincide with the writing standards that spiral in the Common Core State Standards. Over the years, as students explore and practice writing, their sophistication in writing for different purposes and audiences will grow. Students across all grades will learn about and practice opinion/argument, informative/explanatory, and narrative writing.

Purpose and Form

Writers choose specific writing forms to communicate their intended meaning. To choose effectively, they target their purpose and audience before and while they write. Over the years, students will practice writing in different genres to build up a repertoire of writing forms from which to choose. This increasing practice as well as access to information about writing will help students feel more comfortable about writing and, hopefully, enjoy doing it.

In this handbook, the writing forms and models presented coincide primarily with the purposes expressed through the Common Core State Standards. These are to inform, to explain, to narrate, and to persuade. There are other purposes for writing as well, but these four are emphasized to best prepare students for college and career readiness.

TO INFORM The purpose for writing to inform is to share facts and other information. Informational texts such as reports make statements that are supported by facts and truthful evidence.

TO EXPLAIN The purpose for writing to explain is to tell *what, how,* and *why* about a topic. An example is to explain in writing how to do or make something.

TO NARRATE The purpose of writing to narrate is to tell a story. The story can be made up or truthful. Most forms of narrative writing have a beginning, middle, and end. Examples are fictional stories and personal narratives.

TO PERSUADE Writing that has a purpose to persuade states an opinion or goal and supports it with reasons and supporting details in order to get the audience to agree, take action, or both. At Grade 6, the emphasis shifts to argument.

Over the years, as their writing grows more sophisticated, students may find that their purpose for writing is a hybrid of two or more purposes. An example would be literary nonfiction that includes elements of storytelling although it may be written primarily to inform and explain. Another example would be historical fiction that tells a story but relates events accurately in order to inform the reader as well.

Success in School and Life

Students and adults are often judged by how well they can communicate. Students are encouraged to learn to write effectively to be successful in their studies. In particular, by the upper grades, they need to master the basic essay format that includes

- An introductory paragraph that identifies the topic or statement of purpose.

- Supporting paragraphs that provide related details and examples.

Purposes for Writing

A blank page can be intimidating. Luckily, there are many ways to overcome the blank page. One way to plan your writing before you start is to think about your **purpose**, or your main reason for writing. You can determine your purpose by asking yourself, *Why will I write?*

● To Inform

To inform means to share or show information. Sometimes it is meant to instruct or teach. Sometimes it relates interesting facts or details. Some kinds of informative writing are articles, reports, and essays.

● To Explain

To explain means to tell about a topic by describing *what, why,* and *how.* You can explain a topic in any type of writing. Some examples of writing to explain are instructions, science observation reports, and explanations.

● To Narrate

To narrate means to tell a true or fictional story. You might write to amuse, touch, or thrill your reader. You might also write to express thoughts and feelings. Some kinds of writing to narrate are short stories, novels, and personal narratives.

● To Persuade

To persuade means to convince someone else to agree with your opinion or to take action. Examples of writing to persuade include a letter, a speech, an argument, or a review.

Understanding Task, Audience, and Purpose (TAP)

In addition to choosing a purpose for writing, you should consider your **audience**, or for whom you are writing. For example, you might write differently when writing to a friend than when writing to someone you don't know. Think about who will be reading your writing as you plan.

Finally, choose a **task**, or writing form. For example, if you want to persuade your class to do something, you might write a speech, an essay, or make a poster.

Before you begin writing, it is a good idea to decide your task, audience, and purpose, or **TAP**. You may choose your own TAP, or your TAP may be assigned to you.

> **? Ask yourself these questions.**
>
> **Task:** What kind of writing will I do?
> *Do I want to write a poem, a story, a research report, or something else?*
>
> **Audience:** Who will read my writing?
> *Am I writing for a teacher, a friend, a committee, or someone else?*
>
> **Purpose:** Why am I writing?
> *Am I writing to inform, explain, narrate, or persuade?*

● A closing paragraph that sums up and concludes.

Students will use this essay form to produce reports, literary analyses, theses, and critiques throughout their academic career. They will also be tested on their ability to write effective essays in standardized tests. In later life, as adults, they will need to be able to communicate clearly in writing to coworkers, bosses, and clients. This requires extensive and ongoing exposure to exemplary writing models and explicit instruction in a variety of areas, as well as opportunities to practice different forms of writing. In all cases, their purpose for writing must be clear. Evidence suggests that the more time student writers spend on writing, developing their writing skills, and deepening their writing experience, the better writers they become.

The Reading-Writing Connection

The ability to communicate their thinking about texts for a variety of purposes and audiences will serve students well in preparation for college and career readiness. When students write about what they read, reflecting on content, craft, or another aspect of a text, they provide evidence of their thinking. This helps teachers know how well students have understood a text. Additionally, the more students write in response to texts, the more they increase their ability to reflect and improve their critical writing ability. Also, students learn to cite evidence from texts in supporting their claims or supporting their main ideas. This ability becomes particularly useful in writing reports and opinion pieces.

Introduce the Purposes

Have students turn to page 8 and read the text. Explain that these are the key purposes for writing that will be explored in their handbooks. Give or elicit an example of a writing form that might be used for each purpose. Examples might include an informational paragraph or a research report *to inform,* directions or a how-to essay *to explain,* a story or personal narrative *to narrate,* and an opinion essay or letter to the editor *to persuade.* Then have students read the next page. Discuss how students should always consider their TAP—or task, audience, and purpose—to help them better target the message of their writing.

The Writing Process

The *Common Core Writing Handbook* presents the writing process as a strategy that students can use to help them write for any task, audience, or purpose. Students can use the writing process independently or as part of writing workshops in which they respond to each other's writing. The writing process can help students understand how to plan, write, and revise for various purposes and genres. It is thus useful in helping students meet the Common Core State Standards for opinion, informative/explanatory, and narrative writing.

What Process Writing Is

The writing process, or process writing, is an instructional approach to writing that consists of five basic stages. The stages are prewriting, drafting, revising, editing, and publishing. The stages are recursive in nature, meaning that students are encouraged to go back and forth between the stages as needed.

The characteristics of the stages of the writing process are as follows:

Prewriting

This is the stage where students begin to plan their writing. Students:

- Define a task and purpose.
- Identify an audience.
- Brainstorm ideas.
- Narrow and choose a topic.
- Plan and organize information.

Drafting

During drafting, students make their first attempt at fleshing out the prewriting idea and forming it into a written work. In other words, students put their ideas in writing. In this stage, students:

- Write a first draft.
- Do not yet worry about perfecting their writing.

- Know that they can revise, edit, and proofread later.
- Use their plan and checklists to help them write or to return to prewriting, as needed.

Revising

A draft is reread and decisions are made to rework and improve it. In this stage, students might:

- Read aloud their work to others to determine how it sounds and how it might be improved.
- Conference with other students or their teachers.
- Add information.
- Delete unnecessary information.
- Rearrange sentences and paragraphs.
- Combine sentences.

Editing

During editing, the draft is polished. In this stage, students reread and correct their writing for the following:

- Grammar
- Spelling
- Mechanics

The Writing Process

Writing can be like taking a journey through your own imagination. You begin with a destination in mind, but the road you take to get there may not be direct. As you travel, you sometimes make discoveries that lead you in new directions. There is no right or wrong road, but the writing process provides a map to guide you.

As you write, you may choose to exit to another stage in the writing process before continuing. You may choose the same exit more than once. You may pass an exit and return to it later. It's your choice—you, the writer, are in the driver's seat.

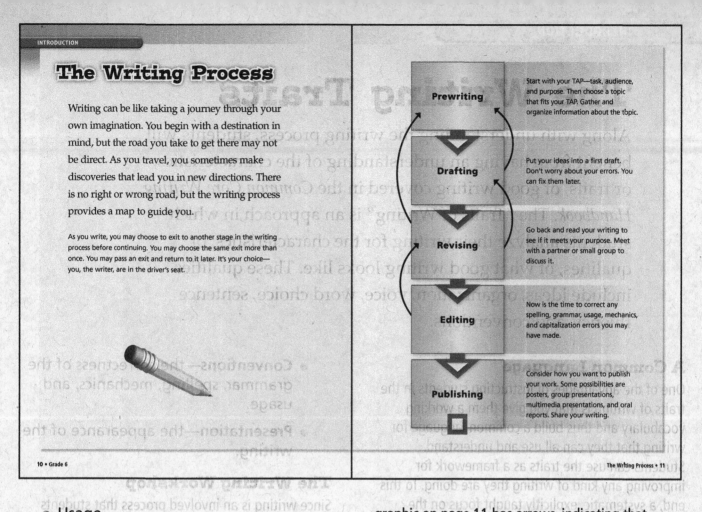

Prewriting — Start with your TAP—task, audience, and purpose. Then choose a topic that fits your TAP. Gather and organize information about the topic.

Drafting — Put your ideas into a first draft. Don't worry about your errors. You can fix them later.

Revising — Go back and read your writing to see if it meets your purpose. Meet with a partner or small group to discuss it.

Editing — Now is the time to correct any spelling, grammar, usage, mechanics, and capitalization errors you may have made.

Publishing — Consider how you want to publish your work. Some possibilities are posters, group presentations, multimedia presentations, and oral reports. Share your writing.

- Usage

Publishing

Students share their writing with others. In this stage, students typically:

- Make a final, clean copy.

- Use their best handwriting, if writing by hand. If they are sharing their work electronically, they typically choose typefaces and other elements to make their writing readable and attractive.

- Combine their writing with art or graphics.

- Make multiple copies, read their writing aloud, post it electronically, or share and display it in some other way.

Introduce the Process

Have students read pages 10–11. Explain that the writing process is a strategy that they can use to help them write about any topic. Point out how the

graphic on page 11 has arrows, indicating that students can go back and forth between the stages as needed. For students who have no previous orientation to the writing process, simplify your introduction by emphasizing at first only the three key stages of planning, drafting, and revising. Elicit how most tasks of any nature require planning, doing or making something, and then thinking about what might be done better and making those improvements. Compare how these same basic stages can be used each time students write.

Have students turn to the table of contents and locate the section in their handbooks devoted to the writing process (pages 74–81). Explain that they can use these handbook pages whenever they need help with specific stages or writing in general. Point out that each stage in the handbook has one or two pages devoted to it that tell more about the stage. As an example, have students turn to the Prewriting pages 74–75, and point out how they show the different organizational plans students can use for the different kinds of writing they will do. Encourage students to use their handbooks as a resource whenever they write.

The Writing Traits

Along with understanding the writing process, students will benefit from having an understanding of the characteristics, or traits, of good writing covered in the *Common Core Writing Handbook*. The "Traits of Writing" is an approach in which students analyze their writing for the characteristics, or qualities, of what good writing looks like. These qualities include ideas, organization, voice, word choice, sentence fluency, and conventions.

A Common Language

One of the advantages of instructing students in the traits of writing is that you give them a working vocabulary and thus build a common language for writing that they can all use and understand. Students can use the traits as a framework for improving any kind of writing they are doing. To this end, a systematic, explicitly taught focus on the traits of writing has proved to be an effective tool for discussing writing, enabling students to analyze and improve their own writing, and providing teachers with a way to assess students' compositions in a fair, even-handed manner.

Writers typically focus on six traits, with presentation—or the appearance of writing— sometimes considered an additional trait.

- **Ideas**—the meaning and development of the message.
- **Organization**—the structure of the writing.
- **Voice**—the tone of the writing, which reveals the writer's personality and affects the audience's interpretation of the message.
- **Word Choice**—the words the writer uses to convey the message.
- **Sentence Fluency**—the flow and rhythm of the writing.

- **Conventions**—the correctness of the grammar, spelling, mechanics, and usage.
- **Presentation**—the appearance of the writing.

The Writing Workshop

Since writing is an involved process that students accomplish at varying speeds, it is usually a good idea to set aside a block of time for them to work on their writing. One time-tested model that has worked well in classrooms is the Writing Workshop. In this model during a set period of time, students work individually and collaboratively (with classmates and/or with the teacher) on different writing activities. One of these activities is for students to collaborate in reviewing each other's manuscripts. One effective technique used in many workshops as a way for students to comment on aspects of each other's writing is to use the language of the traits when they comment.

Some tasks are started and finished during a workshop, while others are ongoing. A writing workshop can serve many writing-related functions:

- Students can work on a class writing assignment (ongoing or quickly accomplished).
- Students can engage in independent writing, jotting down or consulting ideas in their writing log or journal,

The Writing Traits

Good writing keeps you reading from sentence to sentence. How can you tell if your writing is good? All good writing has five traits, or characteristics. Once you understand the traits, you'll know what to look for to make your writing great and keep your readers reading.

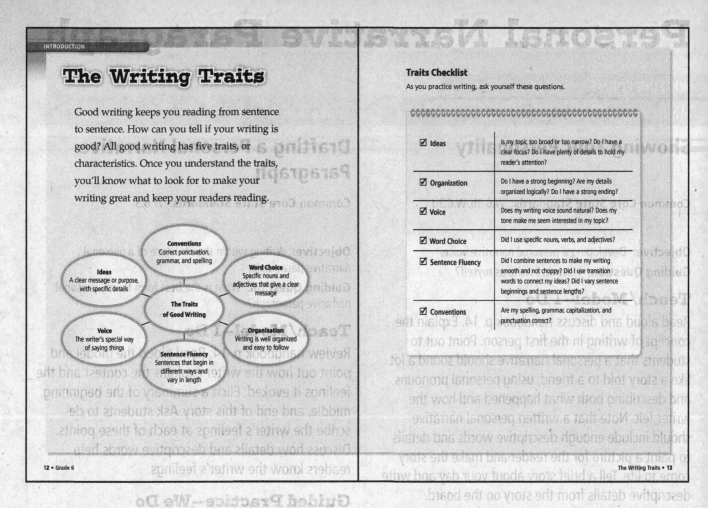

Conventions
Correct punctuation, grammar, and spelling

Word Choice
Specific nouns and adjectives that give a clear message

Ideas
A clear message or purpose, with specific details

The Traits of Good Writing

Voice
The writer's special way of saying things

Organization
Writing is well organized and easy to follow

Sentence Fluency
Sentences that begin in different ways and vary in length

Traits Checklist

As you practice writing, ask yourself these questions.

☑ Ideas	Is my topic too broad or too narrow? Do I have a clear focus? Do I have plenty of details to hold my reader's attention?
☑ Organization	Do I have a strong beginning? Are my details organized logically? Do I have a strong ending?
☑ Voice	Does my writing voice sound natural? Does my tone make me seem interested in my topic?
☑ Word Choice	Did I use specific nouns, verbs, and adjectives?
☑ Sentence Fluency	Did I combine sentences to make my writing smooth and not choppy? Did I use transition words to connect my ideas? Did I vary sentence beginnings and sentence lengths?
☑ Conventions	Are my spelling, grammar, capitalization, and punctuation correct?

starting or working on pieces of their own devising.

- As previously mentioned, students can engage in peer-conferencing, giving one another advice about a piece of writing or sharing writing ideas.

- Students can select pieces for inclusion in their writing portfolio, where they keep their best work.

- Teachers can conference with individual students, reviewing student writing and discussing a given student's strengths and weaknesses as well as instructional progress.

- Teachers can engage in small-group instruction with students who need extra help with practice in specific areas of writing.

Writing Workshops are often most effective when they adhere to a dependable schedule and follow a

set of clearly posted guidelines (for example, keep voices down, point out the good things about someone's writing as well as comment on aspects that might be revised, listen politely, put away materials when the workshop is over). In addition, students should know what areas of the classroom they can use during the Workshop and should have free access to writing materials, including their handbooks.

You may want to refer to the Writing Workshop pages in this *Common Core Writing Handbook Teacher's Guide* and teach one or two minilessons on writing workshop behaviors and activities so that students have a solid understanding of what is expected of them.

Introduce the Traits

Share the Writing Traits overview pages with students. Discuss each trait briefly and explain to students that their handbooks contain more information on the traits, which they can use to help them as they plan, draft, revise, edit, and publish their writing. Guide students to use their tables of contents or indexes to locate where additional information can be found in their handbooks.

Personal Narrative Paragraph

Minilesson 1

Showing Your Personality

Common Core State Standards: W.6.3b, W.6.3d

Objective: Developing a personal narrative voice.
Guiding Question: How do I write as myself?

Teach/Model—I Do

Read aloud and discuss handbook p. 14. Explain the concept of writing in the first person. Point out to students that a personal narrative should sound a lot like a story told to a friend, using personal pronouns and describing both what happened and how the writer felt. Note that a written personal narrative should include enough descriptive words and details to paint a picture for the reader and make the story come to life. Tell a brief story about your day and write descriptive details from the story on the board.

Guided Practice—We Do

Choose a character from a story the class has read. Work together to find examples from the story that show the character's personality. Guide students to write down descriptive details about the character.

Practice/Apply—You Do

COLLABORATIVE Have pairs tell each other stories about something that happened this week. Tell them that, as they speak, they should write down descriptive details that show their own personality. Then have students exchange papers and discuss the descriptive details they used.

INDEPENDENT Have students think about something that happened to them this summer. Have them write a list of descriptive details they can use to tell the story that show their personality.

Conference/Evaluate

Circulate and help students choose details that are both descriptive and show their personality.

Minilesson 2

Drafting a Personal Narrative Paragraph

Common Core State Standards: W.6.3

Objective: Writing within the structure of a personal narrative paragraph.
Guiding Question: What is the best form for my personal narrative paragraph?

Teach/Model—I Do

Review handbook p. 14. Read aloud the model and point out how the writer explains the contest and the feelings it evoked. Elicit a summary of the beginning, middle, and end of this story. Ask students to describe the writer's feelings at each of these points. Discuss how details and descriptive words help readers know the writer's feelings.

Guided Practice—We Do

 Direct students to the frame on handbook p. 15. Tell students that you will work with them to write a personal narrative about a good day at school. Using the frame, elicit suggestions for things that could have happened to the narrator to make a really good day, such as *First, we had a special visitor.* Have students write in their books as you write on the board.

Practice/Apply—You Do

 COLLABORATIVE Ask groups to plan and complete Activity 2. Have students in each group work together to write about the event they discussed earlier, or to choose a new exciting event.

 INDEPENDENT Have students read and follow the directions. Have them use their plans from Lesson 1 or another plan they create using Graphic Organizer 4.

Conference/Evaluate

As students draft, have them evaluate their work using the rubric on p. 104.

Personal Narrative Paragraph

A **personal narrative paragraph** is a narrative about an experience from the writer's own life told from the first-person, "I," point of view.

Parts of a Personal Narrative Paragraph
- An opening sentence to introduce the topic and grab the reader's attention
- Details and actions presented in logical order
- Details that explain thoughts and feelings about the event, using the word "I"
- Vivid descriptions to help the reader picture what happened

Beginning
Grabs the reader's attention

Events
Actions in time order

Vivid Details
Show what happened and how the author felt

Ending
Shows the author's reaction to the event

My heart raced when our teacher announced the rules for the writing contest. I'd always wanted to be a professional writer, but I'd never told anyone because I didn't think I was good enough. This was my chance to prove myself and have my own story published in a literary journal. I went straight home **after** school and got to work. I already knew exactly what I wanted to write about. The characters seemed to be **flying out of my head,** and I couldn't write fast enough. I finished my final draft just **before** Dad made me go to bed. **My mind jumped** between excitement and worry. I knew it was my best story yet, but was it good enough? Did I have any chance at all? My **hands shook** when I turned in the manuscript the next morning. I didn't know how I could wait an entire week to find out if I had won. When the day **finally** came, I couldn't focus in class or eat anything at lunch. My fingers rapidly tapped the top of the desk at the beginning of 6th period **while** I sat waiting for the announcement. When the principal's crackling voice said my name over the PA system, I could have jumped as high as the ceiling. Perhaps I had what it took to become a writer after all.

Other Transitions
First
Later
Eventually
After
Next
Following

Follow your teacher's directions to complete this page.

1 My favorite day at school was when _____
_____ First, _____

Then, _____
_____
_____

The best part was _____
_____
_____
_____
_____
_____

Eventually _____
_____
_____

2 On a separate sheet of paper, write a personal narrative paragraph about a time when you got to do something exciting.

3 On a separate sheet of paper, use your prewriting plan to write a personal narrative paragraph, or make a new plan that tells about a time when you were afraid.

✓ Corrective Feedback

IF . . . students are having a hard time coming up with enough details,

THEN . . . have them imagine that particular moment in the narrative and then write down things they might have seen, heard, smelled, felt, or thought. Have students pick the most compelling of these new details and add them to the narrative.

Focus Trait: Voice

One important characteristic of a personal narrative is that it is personal; no two personal narratives should be the same, even if they are about the same event.

Ask students to think about how they can express their individual voice in a personal narrative. Discuss which tools they can use, such as descriptions of their thoughts or feelings, to focus the narrative on their own experience of an event. Explain that while

the sequence of events is very important in a personal narrative, the writer's feelings and thoughts about the events are just as important. Model this by rereading the model story from p. 14 while omitting the sentences about the writer's feelings and thoughts. Discuss the differences between the two versions, helping students understand how the printed model gives a fuller, more personal version of the events.

Personal Narrative

Minilesson 3

Turning Memories Into Stories

Common Core State Standards: W.6.3a, W.6.3b, W.6.3d, W.6.3e

Objective: Sequencing a real event into a story structure.

Guiding Question: How do I turn my memory into a story?

Teach/Model—I Do

Read aloud and discuss handbook p. 16. Discuss the basic structure of a story: beginning, middle, and end. Point out that real life often isn't that clear. Explain that it can be a challenge for a writer to identify good places to start or stop a story. Mention that the events in the model are shown in the order they happened.

Guided Practice—We Do

Work with students to come up with ideas for a personal narrative, such as playing a sport or learning a musical instrument. Guide students to come up with a few events for the narrative, such as *I wanted to play baseball, but I wasn't very good. I tried soccer instead.* Work together to write the events of the narrative in order.

Practice/Apply—You Do

COLLABORATIVE Ask small groups to plan a story about their day at school. Have students work together to come up with a few different events for the story. Then have them work together to put the events of the story in order.

INDEPENDENT Have students brainstorm ideas for events in a personal narrative about a time they accomplished something they were proud of. Have them write the events in order.

Conference/Evaluate

Have students evaluate their outlines and decide if they chose the most interesting points for focus.

Minilesson 4

Drafting a Personal Narrative

Common Core State Standards: W.6.3a, W.6.3b, W.6.3d, W.6.3e

Objective: Understand the structure of a personal narrative.

Guiding Question: What is the best form for my narrative?

Teach/Model—I Do

Review handbook p. 16. Point out the ways in which the model writer shares the experience of learning music by including details about what happened and her thoughts and feelings. Discuss how this paragraph establishes why the reader should care about the writer's struggle to find the right instrument. Point out how the exclamations help show the writer's personality.

Guided Practice—We Do

 Direct students to the frame on handbook p. 17. Tell students that together you will write a personal narrative about a great holiday. Elicit suggestions for things that might make a holiday great, and write them on the board. As a class, choose the best ideas to complete the frame. Have students write in their books as you write on the board.

Practice/Apply—You Do

 COLLABORATIVE Have groups plan and complete Activity 2. Suggest that they choose one person's idea for a time when they lost something and then work together to brainstorm how to make that into a story.

 INDEPENDENT Have students read and follow the directions. Tell them to use their prewriting plan from Lesson 2 or to brainstorm a new plan using Graphic Organizer 11.

Conference/Evaluate

As students draft, have them evaluate their work using the rubric on p. 104.

Digital
• eBook
• WriteSmart
• Interactive Lessons

Personal Narrative

A **personal narrative** describes an event or theme in the life of the writer. It explains why that event is important.

Parts of a Personal Narrative

- A clear beginning, middle, and end to the story
- Details about how the writer felt during the events and how the writer felt afterward
- An ending that shows the story's importance to the writer

Beginning
Grabs the reader's attention

Details
Show thoughts and feelings

Ending
Tells how the reader felt about what happened

I used to hate practicing music. My mother made me take piano lessons every Saturday morning starting when I was eight. My little brother was allowed to stay home watching cartoons, but I had to go to Mrs. Finklestein's and learn the piano. Sometimes I would pretend to be sick, but that didn't work too well. "If you're too sick for piano, then you're too sick to go out and play," said my mother. So I went to Mrs. Finklestein's.

It wasn't that I didn't like music. I *loved* music. But I didn't love the music I had to play on the piano. There was so much counting! On the piano, I had to count every beat, and I had no control over the sound. I could bang a piano key loudly or tap it quietly, but I couldn't change if it sounded pretty or angry or sad. Also, our piano was old, so most of the notes sounded dull except the F-sharp, which didn't sound at all.

Everything changed last October when my mom put on an old jazz record. I loved it! Every note sounded different, and I couldn't predict what would happen next. My mom said the musician was Miles Davis, and he played the trumpet.

Well guess what? Now I play the trumpet in the school band. And I love practicing music!

Other Transitions
First
Next
Later
Then
Also

16 • Grade 6

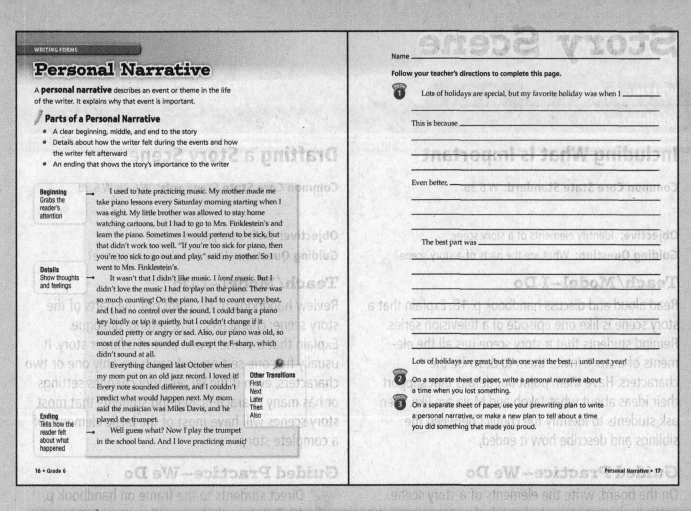

Name _____

Follow your teacher's directions to complete this page.

1 Lots of holidays are special, but my favorite holiday was when I _____
_____

This is because _____
_____
_____

Even better, _____
_____
_____

The best part was _____
_____
_____

Lots of holidays are great, but this one was the best... until next year!

2 On a separate sheet of paper, write a personal narrative about a time when you lost something.

3 On a separate sheet of paper, use your prewriting plan to write a personal narrative, or make a new plan to tell about a time you did something that made you proud.

Personal Narrative • 17

Corrective Feedback

IF . . . students are struggling to determine a beginning, middle, and end to their story,

THEN . . . have them ask themselves "what happened first? next? next?" until they reach the end of the story. Then they should cut out or combine as many of their responses as they can until they are left with an effective order of events for their story.

Focus Trait: Voice

Remind students that personal narratives should sound the way the writer talks. Students may struggle with writing in a personal voice instead of an academic voice. Explain that a personal narrative is not like a history essay. Although writers should follow all the conventions of written English, they can be more casual than in an essay or report.

Have students tell a story about themselves to a partner. If possible, have the partner record the story or, if appropriate equipment is not available, take notes while the story is being told. Then have both students go back over the story and identify where the teller used personal language that established his or her personality (for example, by using a lot of exclamations, recounting specific dialogue, and so on). The teller should make note of these and try to use them in his or her written personal narrative. Have the partners reverse and do the same exercise for the recording partner.

Story Scene

Minilesson 5	Minilesson 6

Including What Is Important

Common Core State Standard: W.6.3b

Objective: Identify elements of a story scene.
Guiding Question: What are the parts of a story scene?

Teach/Model—I Do

Read aloud and discuss handbook p. 18. Explain that a story scene is like one episode of a television series. Remind students that a story scene has all the elements of a story. Invite them to describe the characters. Have them point out details that support their ideas about what Jakob and Maia are like. Then ask students to identify the conflict between the siblings and describe how it ended.

Guided Practice—We Do

On the board, write the elements of a story scene: *setting, characters,* and *plot.* Ask *If a story were set in the Wild West, who might the characters be? What conflict would you expect? What if the setting moved to Antarctica?* Guide students to choose the setting, characters, and plot for a story. Write their responses on the board. Point out that students can begin planning a story scene with any element, but choosing a setting can be an easy place to start.

Practice/Apply—You Do

COLLABORATIVE Ask students to work in groups to choose a setting, characters, and plot for the story. Have them write a list. Then have each group choose a spokesperson to share a summary of their ideas with the class.

INDEPENDENT Challenge students to plan a story scene that could be part of a longer story or series. Ask them to list their ideas for setting, character, and plot.

Conference/Evaluate

Circulate and help students make sure they have included all of the important parts of a story scene.

Drafting a Story Scene

Common Core State Standards: W.6.3b, W.6.3d

Objective: Draft a story scene.
Guiding Question: How do I plan a story scene?

Teach/Model—I Do

Review handbook p. 18. Point out the parts of the story scene: characters, plot, setting, dialogue. Explain that a scene is one part of a larger story. It usually has one setting and can have only one or two characters, even if the larger story changes settings or has many characters. Remind students that most story scenes will have most of the basic elements of a complete story.

Guided Practice—We Do

 Direct students to the frame on handbook p. 19. Tell them that you will write a story scene together. Work together to come up with characters, plot, and setting for a story that takes place on a sunny day. Begin by stating the conflict. For example, *The bright noon sun beat down on us as we walked to the beach. Soon it was starting to look like it might rain.* Work together to complete the frame. Have students write in their books as you write on the board.

Practice/Apply—You Do

 COLLABORATIVE Have groups plan and complete Activity 2. Tell them they may role play their dialogue before they write it down. Have groups share what they have written.

 INDEPENDENT Have students read and follow the directions. Tell them to use their prewriting plan from Lesson 3 or to brainstorm a new plan using Graphic Organizer 10.

Conference/Evaluate

As students draft, have them evaluate their work using the rubric on p. 104.

Story Scene

A **story scene** is a brief fictional narrative of one event that is part of a longer story.

Parts of a Story Scene

- Opening that introduces characters and setting
- Parts of the plot
- Events told in order
- Details and dialogue bring the scene to life

Beginning
Introduces characters and setting

"That should do it." Jakob sighed as he added the last tiny piece to his model of the Colosseum. After weeks of painstaking work, his social studies project was finally done.

"Jakob!" **hollered** Maia, "Dinner!" His door opened.

"No!" Jakob **yelled**, vaulting across his room. "No one is allowed in until I take my Colosseum to school!"

"But I want to see," Maia whined.

"Absolutely not!" Jakob **said**. Ignoring his sister's protests, he closed the door and headed downstairs.

Middle
Describes events in time order

Jakob returned to his room after dinner. He froze when he saw his door open a tiny crack.

"MAIA!" Jakob's voice exploded through the house. He was horrified to find the model covered with drawings of miniature people.

"Do you like it?" Maia grinned from the door. "The Colosseum was a type of theatre, right? And every theatre needs an audience."

Other Dialogue Tags
Grumbled
Suggested
Whispered
Sang
Asked
Wondered

Dialogue and Description
Bring characters and actions to life

Jakob's head fell into his hands. The project was due tomorrow, so there was no time to cover over the drawings. He glared at his little sister, but her bright eyes slowly melted away his remaining anger. At least there was no real damage done.

"Well, I guess they are kind of appropriate," he **admitted**. "I just hope Mrs. Dasho has a sense of humor."

18 • Grade 6

Name _____

Follow your teacher's directions to complete this page.

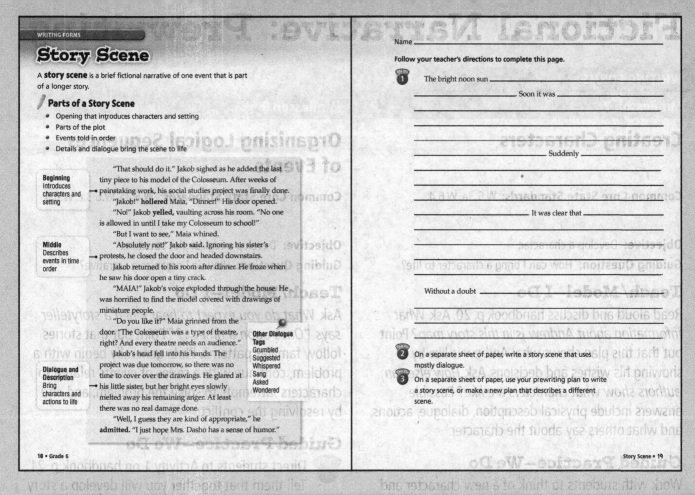

1 The bright noon sun _____

Soon it was _____

_____

_____

_____

Suddenly _____

_____

•

_____

It was clear that _____

_____

Without a doubt _____

_____

2 On a separate sheet of paper, write a story scene that uses mostly dialogue.

3 On a separate sheet of paper, use your prewriting plan to write a story scene, or make a new plan that describes a different scene.

Story Scene • 19

Corrective Feedback

IF . . . students are having a hard time coming up with a plan for their story scene,

THEN . . . suggest that they start with a familiar story and give it a twist. For example, *What would happen if Red Riding Hood was smarter than the wolf? What would "Goldilocks" be like if Goldilocks didn't disturb the bears' things and simply waited for them to return home?*

Focus Trait: Word Choice

Tell students that they can use dialogue tags to bring their characters to life. A *dialogue tag* is a short phrase that identifies a speaker, such as "he said" or "she asked."

Direct students' attention to the dialogue tags in the model on p. 18. Ask them what they learn about Maia from words like *hollered* and *whined*. What does the word *grinned* suggest about her motive for drawing on Jakob's model? Invite them to brainstorm tags the author could have used to suggest that Maia was a

different type of character—perhaps bossy, shy, impatient, or calm.

Dialogue tags can do more than indicate a character's tone of voice. Words like *whispered*, *gasped*, and *nagged* show action. Ask students to identify words that show action from the dialogue tags box on p. 18.

Encourage them to use creative dialogue tags for times when they want to give special emphasis to the way a character speaks.

Fictional Narrative: Prewriting

Minilesson 7

Creating Characters

Common Core State Standards: W.6.3a, W.6.4

Objective: Develop a character.

Guiding Question: How can I bring a character to life?

Teach/Model—I Do

Read aloud and discuss handbook p. 20. Ask *What information about Andrew is in this story map?* Point out that this plan shows what Andrew is like by showing his wishes and decisions. Ask *How else can authors show what characters are like?* Possible answers include physical description, dialogue, actions, and what others say about the character.

Guided Practice—We Do

Work with students to think of a new character and write the character's name on the board. Remind students that authors can use specific details to bring their characters to life. Have them make a list of that character's traits. For example: *James: red hair, freckles, friendly, likes dogs*.

Practice/Apply—You Do

COLLABORATIVE Have partners create a new character and write 3–5 details about that character.

INDEPENDENT Have students work on their own to write 3 additional details about a character they've already created, or have them create a new character and write down 3 details.

Conference/Evaluate

Have students review their list to see whether the details they have included make their character seem like a real person.

Minilesson 8

Organizing Logical Sequences of Events

Common Core State Standards: W.6.3a, W.6.3.c, W.6.4

Objective: Develop a logical plot structure.

Guiding Question: How do I organize a narrative?

Teach/Model—I Do

Ask *What do you expect to hear when a storyteller says "Once upon a time…?"* Point out that stories follow familiar patterns. Plots generally begin with a problem, continue with a series of events related to characters' attempts to solve the problem, and end by resolving the conflict.

Guided Practice—We Do

 Direct students to Activity 1 on handbook p. 21. Tell them that together you will develop a story map. Point out the setting and characters. Work with students to think of names for each of the characters. Then come up with a conflict, such as *Aviva couldn't decide on the most important wish to make on her new magic lamp*. Guide students to choose events for their story and to think of how characters solve the problem. Work together to complete the activity. Have students write in their books as you write on the board.

Practice/Apply—You Do

 COLLABORATIVE Have partners plan and complete Activity 2. Tell them to use words like *first, next,* and *afterward* to show the order in which events happened.

 INDEPENDENT Have students read and follow the directions. Tell them to use their prewriting plan from Lesson 4 or to brainstorm a new plan using Graphic Organizer 10.

Conference/Evaluate

As students draft, have them evaluate their work using the rubric on p. 104.

Fictional Narrative: Prewriting

A **fictional narrative** is an imaginative story with characters and a plot. It has a beginning, a middle, and an ending.

Parts of a Fictional Narrative

- A plot with events told in sequential, or time, order
- A setting, or when and where the story takes place
- A problem, or conflict, that the characters must solve
- An ending, or resolution, that wraps up the story

Title: Andrew Wants a Pet

Setting: current day, Andrew's room	**Characters:** Andrew, talking pet goldfish
Plot	

Problem (Conflict): Andrew wants a pet, but his house is too small for a dog and his mom is allergic to cats.

Events: Andrew wishes for a bigger house, and his fish grants the wish. Andrew doesn't like cleaning the big house, so his fish makes it smaller again. Andrew wishes away his mom's cat allergy, but then he is allergic to cats.

Ending (Resolution): Andrew is satisfied with having a talking fish for a pet.

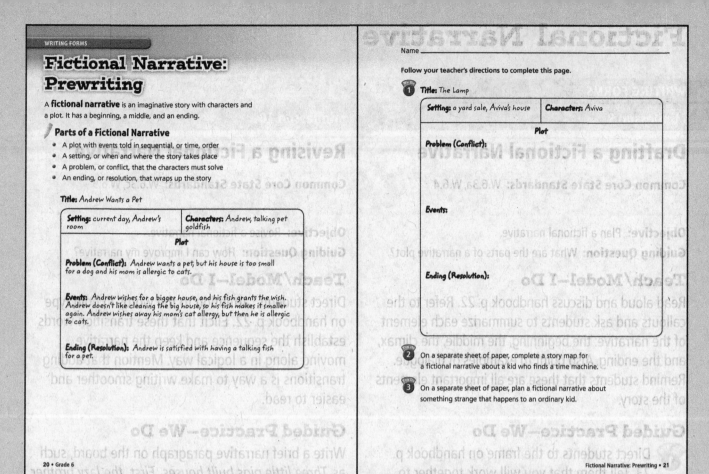

Name _____

Follow your teacher's directions to complete this page.

1 **Title:** The Lamp

Setting: a yard sale, Aviva's house	**Characters:** Aviva
Plot	

Problem (Conflict):

Events:

Ending (Resolution):

2 On a separate sheet of paper, complete a story map for a fictional narrative about a kid who finds a time machine.

3 On a separate sheet of paper, plan a fictional narrative about something strange that happens to an ordinary kid.

Corrective Feedback

IF . . . students find it difficult to create a character,

THEN . . . ask them to think of an actor who could play the character. Encourage them to use what they know of the actor's appearance and personality to develop their imaginary character.

Focus Trait: Organization

Remind students that narratives usually follow time order; that is, events are presented in the sequence in which they happened.

Words that signal time order include *first*, *later*, *soon*, and *finally*. Ask students to suggest other time signals, such as *in the beginning* or *meanwhile*. List their suggestions on the board.

Then work with the class to add transitions to the beginning of each sentence in the plot summary on p. 20. For example, *In the beginning, Andrew wants a pet….First, Andrew wishes for a bigger house.*

Fictional Narrative

Minilesson 9

Drafting a Fictional Narrative

Common Core State Standards: W.6.3a, W.6.4

Objective: Plan a fictional narrative.
Guiding Question: What are the parts of a narrative plot?

Teach/Model—I Do

Read aloud and discuss handbook p. 22. Refer to the callouts and ask students to summarize each element of the narrative: the beginning, the middle, the climax, and the ending. Also point to examples of dialogue. Remind students that these are all important elements of the story.

Guided Practice—We Do

 Direct students to the frame on handbook p. 23. Tell them that you will work together to write a fictional narrative. Discuss what might happen if someone found a magic lamp. Guide children to write the first sentence in the frame, such as *Suddenly a cloud of dust whooshed out of the lamp*. Then complete the frame together. Have students write in their books as you write on the board.

Practice/Apply—You Do

 COLLABORATIVE Have partners plan and complete Activity 2. Tell them they can use their plan from the previous lesson.

 INDEPENDENT Have students read and follow the directions for Activity 3. Tell them to use their prewriting plan from the previous lesson or to create a new plan.

Conference/Evaluate

As students draft, have them evaluate their work using the rubric on p. 104.

Minilesson 10

Revising a Fictional Narrative

Common Core State Standards: W.6.3c, W.6.5

Objective: Revise a fictional narrative.
Guiding Question: How can I improve my narrative?

Teach/Model—I Do

Direct students' attention to the words in bold type on handbook p. 22. Elicit that these transition words establish the sequence and keep the narrative moving along in a logical way. Mention that adding transitions is a way to make writing smoother and easier to read.

Guided Practice—We Do

Write a brief narrative paragraph on the board, such as *Three little pigs built houses. First, the lazy brother built one of straw. Next, the middle brother built one of sticks. The youngest brother took time to think and finally built his from bricks. The big bad wolf came.* Work with students to mark the transitions that help readers follow the order of the plot: *first, next,* and *finally.* Ask *Where else is a transition needed? How could we change the last sentence to make the order of events more clear?*

Practice/Apply—You Do

COLLABORATIVE Ask partners to choose one of their drafts from Minilesson 9 and work together to find places to add transition words.

INDEPENDENT Have students choose a draft to revise. If they have included enough transitions, encourage them to find other ways to revise their drafts using the rubric on p. 104 as a guide.

Conference/Evaluate

Have students review their revised drafts to be sure the drafts flow smoothly from the beginning through the middle and climax to the ending.

- eBook
- WriteSmart
- Interactive Lessons

Fictional Narrative

A **fictional narrative** is an imaginative story with characters and a plot. It has a beginning, a middle, and an ending.

Parts of a Fictional Narrative

- A plot that is usually told in time order, or sequence
- Details and dialogue that make the events and characters seem real
- A conflict, or problem, that the characters must solve
- A climax, or high point, that shows how the characters solve the problem
- An ending that wraps up the story

Beginning
Introduces the characters, setting, and problem

Middle
Contains details and dialogue that make characters seem real

Climax
Shows how the character solves the problem

Ending
Wraps up the story

Andrew wanted a pet more than anything. His mother told him that their house was too small for a dog, and she was allergic to cats. All Andrew had was a goldfish in a glass bowl.

Alone in his room with his fish, Andrew muttered, "I wish our house were bigger!" **Suddenly**, it was. In fact, it was huge!

"Be careful what you wish for," the goldfish said. As much as Andrew wanted a dog, his chore—vacuuming—would have taken all of his time and energy.

"Okay, I wish the house were small again," he told the goldfish. **Right away**, the house changed back.

"One more wish, you foolish boy," the goldfish warned.

"Okay," Andrew said, "I wish my mom weren't allergic to cats!" **The next day**, Andrew brought home a cat. His mother was fine, but Andrew started to sneeze and couldn't stop. He had to give the cat to a friend. **At last**, he gave up.

"All right, you win," he told the fish. "No more wishes. I guess a fish that talks isn't the worst pet in the world!"

Other Transitions
At first
After a while
During
Later
Before long
Finally
In the end

22 • Grade 6

Name _____

Follow your teacher's directions to complete this page.

1 Aviva never thought she would have an adventure—until the day she found the strange-looking lamp at a yard sale. She brought it home and rubbed it with a cloth. Suddenly _____

_____

Right away, _____

_____

The next day, _____

_____

Later on, _____

_____

Before long, _____

_____

In the end, _____

2 On a separate sheet of paper, write a fictional narrative about a character who finds a time machine.

3 On a separate sheet of paper, use your prewriting plan to write a fictional narrative, or plan and write a story about something strange that happens to an ordinary kid.

✓ Corrective Feedback

IF . . . students find it difficult to sequence their plot in a logical order,

THEN . . . ask them to write down, in no particular order, everything that might happen in their narrative. Have students choose the events they want to include in the narrative and then place each of those events on a timeline.

Focus Trait: Word Choice

Transitions such as *first*, *next*, and *last* are effective ways to show time order. However, they are also predictable.

Write this sentence on the board:

Andrew wished his house were bigger. Then it was.

Change the word *then* to *suddenly*. Ask *Which transition is most effective?*

Write this sentence on the board: *Andrew gave up.*

Then add *At last* to the beginning of the sentence. Ask *How does this transition give more meaning to the sentence?*

Remind students that transitions can do more than show time order. Choosing words like *suddenly* or *incredibly* can also create surprise or emotional impact.

Response Paragraph

Minilesson 11	**Minilesson 12**

Analyzing Literature

Common Core State Standard: W.6.9

Objective: Draw conclusions about theme.

Guiding Question: What is the theme of this story?

Teach/Model—I Do

With students, read aloud and discuss handbook p. 24. Explain that, in a response paragraph, the writer analyzes something he or she has read. The writer identifies all the important parts of the text—characters, setting, plot, and so on—and uses those details to draw conclusions and make connections. Explain how the writer's plot summary in the model supports the theme of self-discovery: Kim's many experiences help him realize that he is a "mixture o' things."

Guided Practice—We Do

With students, review the story "Science Friction" or another story the class has read. Guide students to write one theme of the story, such as *Sometimes people's shortcomings are actually what make them special.* Then work with students to select plot details and quotations that support the theme. (Example: *At first, Amanda is annoyed that Ellen is so organized, but Amanda appreciates Ellen's neatness when Ellen makes beautiful signs for the report.*) Write their suggestions on the board, and save them to use in Minilesson 12.

Practice/Apply—You Do

COLLABORATIVE Have groups choose another book or story and repeat the exercise above. Remind them that, when they draw a conclusion, they should use what the author has written to support their idea.

INDEPENDENT Have students choose a new book or story and repeat the exercise on their own.

Conference/Evaluate

Circulate, making sure that students' plot details and quotations support the theme.

Drafting a Response Paragraph

Common Core State Standard: W.6.9

Objective: Write a response paragraph that demonstrates understanding of theme, character, plot, and setting.

Guiding Question: How do the characters, plot, and setting relate to the theme?

Teach/Model—I Do

Review with students handbook p. 24. Read aloud the student model, pointing out how details about the characters, plot, and setting support the writer's interpretation of the book's theme. Explain that setting is important to the theme of Kim's discovery that he is a "mixture o' things": Kim is Irish but lives in a different culture in India. His experiences with the monk and at the British school also show two sides of his character. Tell students that, in their own response essays, they should include details and quotations from the story to support their ideas.

Guided Practice—We Do

 Direct students to the frame on handbook p. 25. Display the class's notes about the theme and plot of "Science Friction" from Minilesson 11. Help students complete the opening with one or two sentences that clearly state the theme. Then work together to complete the rest of the frame with details and quotations that show how the theme relates to the story. Write on the board as students write in their books.

Practice/Apply—You Do

 COLLABORATIVE Have groups select another book or story and complete Activity 2. Remind them to make connections to their own lives. Tell groups to share what they have written.

 INDEPENDENT Have students read and follow the directions.

Conference/Evaluate

Have students evaluate their essays using the rubric on p. 104.

Response Paragraph

A **response paragraph** tells how the writer feels about a piece of literature that he or she has read. The writer interprets the work and draws a conclusion about it.

Parts of a Response Paragraph

- An opening that clearly states the writer's main idea about the original text
- A brief summary of the characters, setting, and plot
- Examples and quotations from the text
- A closing that restates the writer's idea and connects the text to the writer's own life

Opening Sentence States the writer's main idea or opinion	Rudyard Kipling's *Kim* is an adventure story, but it is also a story about growing up and finding out who you are. **The story is about** Kim, an Irish orphan living in Lahore, India. Kim joins a monk on a spiritual journey because Kim wants to learn from him. As they travel, Kim is taken from the monk and educated in a British school. At school, he becomes a British spy. **Then** he graduates and reunites with the monk. They journey to the Himalayan Mountains. They are both hurt in an exciting battle with French and Russian spies. Luckily, Kim gets important maps from the spies. **After** Kim and the monk get better, Kim helps the monk reach his goal. Through these adventures, Kim discovers that he is "a mixture o' things." He is not completely Indian and not completely British. Like Kim, I am a mixture of things. I am like my father in some ways and like my mother in others. I also have my own interests and feelings. Kim has an exciting life in a faraway country, but we are alike because we have to find our true selves.
Summary Tells writer's opinions about the characters, setting, and plot	
Examples and quotations	
Closing Restates the main idea	

Other Words for Responding
In the book
The plot starts
The first thing
Next
The best part
One similarity
In my opinion

Follow your teacher's directions to complete this page.

 "Science Friction," by David Lubar, is a very funny story. _____
_____
_____ The story is about _____
_____

_____ Then _____
_____
_____
_____
_____ After _____
_____
_____ I think _____

 On a separate sheet of paper, write a response paragraph about a book, story, or play that inspired you. Remember to include examples from the text about the characters, setting, and plot.

On a separate sheet of paper, use your prewriting plan to write a response paragraph, or make a new plan to write about your favorite book, short story, or play.

Corrective Feedback

IF . . . students need help identifying character, setting, and plot events for the summary part of their responses,

THEN . . . have them use a story map like Graphic Organizer 10 to note the most important story elements. They can write the setting in the upper left-hand box and the characters in the upper right-hand box. Then they can choose events in the story to use in a plot summary in the large box below. Once they have mapped out the entire story, they can decide which elements they want to focus on in their essays.

Focus Trait: Word Choice

Remind students that, even when they are describing an author's work, they can only use the author's exact language if they put it in quotation marks. Any other statements about a selection should be rephrased in the student's own words.

Provide an example sentence taken from an author's work, such as the following:

"Aunt Helga was a stately presence in the family, a quiet anchor in a raging sea."

Then show students two possible ways to reference this description in a response to literature:

Aunt Helga is described as "a quiet anchor in a raging sea."

Aunt Helga is a calm, supportive figure in her family.

Argument Paragraph

Introducing and Supporting Claims

Common Core State Standards: W.6.1a, W.6.1b

Objective: Develop and support a claim.

Guiding Question: What are the parts of an argument?

Teach/Model—I Do

Read aloud and discuss handbook p. 26. Emphasize that the first sentence states *what* the author thinks about the topic. The rest of the paragraph focuses on *why* readers should agree. Ask students to identify the evidence provided and discuss whether different audiences, such as students and teachers, would find it convincing.

Guided Practice—We Do

Work with students to brainstorm a list of extracurricular activities they'd like to see added to the school, such as *literary magazine* or *martial arts*. On the board, draw a 2-column chart with *Claim* written at the top of the first column and *Reasons* in the second. Work with students to complete the chart with ideas for at least three argument paragraphs, such as *add martial arts classes* and *good way for students to have fun and get more exercise*.

Practice/Apply—You Do

COLLABORATIVE Have groups choose another activity from the list. Tell them to draw a chart like the one on the board and then write an argument and at least two reasons or pieces of supporting evidence. Have groups discuss whether each other's evidence is persuasive.

INDEPENDENT Have students choose another activity from the list or come up with a new topic. Have them make a chart like the one on the board with their argument and at least two reasons.

Conference/Evaluate

Work with students to determine whether their reasons make sense and that their evidence is related to the argument.

Drafting an Argument Paragraph

Common Core State Standards: W.6.1a, W.6.1b

Objective: Draft an argument paragraph.

Guiding Question: How do I plan an argument paragraph?

Teach/Model—I Do

Ask students how they react when someone says they should believe or do something *because I said so*. Have them review the callouts on p. 26. Ask *What is the difference between writing an argument paragraph and saying* because I said so? Point out that the model writer gives reasons and evidence to support the argument.

Guided Practice—We Do

 Direct students to the frame on handbook p. 27. Tell them that you will write an argument paragraph together. Work together to develop an argument to open the paragraph, such as *We believe it is important for students to be able to have many after-school activity options.* Work with students to brainstorm reasons and supporting evidence. Complete the frame by putting the evidence in a logical order, such as least to most important. Have students write in their books as you write on the board.

Practice/Apply—You Do

 COLLABORATIVE Have groups plan and complete Activity 2. Remind them that their evidence should be convincing to both students and teachers. Have groups share what they have written.

 INDEPENDENT Have students read and follow the directions. Tell them to use their prewriting plan from Lesson 7 or to brainstorm a new plan using Graphic Organizer 7.

Conference/Evaluate

As students draft, have them evaluate their work using the rubric on p. 104.

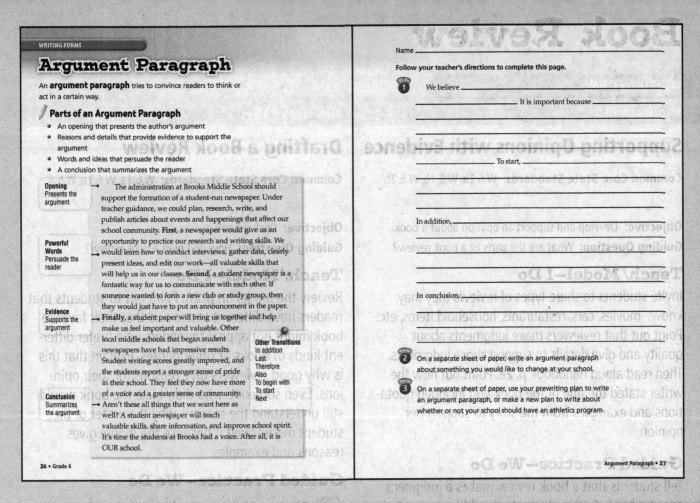

Argument Paragraph

An **argument paragraph** tries to convince readers to think or act in a certain way.

Parts of an Argument Paragraph

- An opening that presents the author's argument
- Reasons and details that provide evidence to support the argument
- Words and ideas that persuade the reader
- A conclusion that summarizes the argument

Opening
Presents the argument

Powerful Words
Persuade the reader

Evidence
Supports the argument

Conclusion
Summarizes the argument

> The administration at Brooks Middle School should support the formation of a student-run newspaper. Under teacher guidance, we could plan, research, write, and publish articles about events and happenings that affect our school community. **First,** a newspaper would give us an opportunity to practice our research and writing skills. We would learn how to conduct interviews, gather data, clearly present ideas, and edit our work—all valuable skills that will help us in our classes. **Second,** a student newspaper is a fantastic way for us to communicate with each other. If someone wanted to form a new club or study group, then they would just have to put an announcement in the paper. **Finally,** a student paper will bring us together and help make us feel important and valuable. Other local middle schools that began student newspapers have had impressive results. Student writing scores greatly improved, and the students report a stronger sense of pride in their school. They feel they now have more of a voice and a greater sense of community. Aren't these all things that we want here as well? A student newspaper will teach valuable skills, share information, and improve school spirit. It's time the students at Brooks had a voice. After all, it is OUR school.

Other Transitions
In addition
Last
Therefore
Also
To begin with
To start
Next

Name _____

Follow your teacher's directions to complete this page.

1 We believe _____

_____ It is important because _____

_____

_____ To start, _____

_____

_____

In addition, _____

_____

In conclusion, _____

_____

2 On a separate sheet of paper, write an argument paragraph about something you would like to change at your school.

3 On a separate sheet of paper, use your prewriting plan to write an argument paragraph, or make a new plan to write about whether or not your school should have an athletics program.

✔ Corrective Feedback

IF . . . students are having a hard time developing an argument,

THEN . . . suggest that they ask a question about their topic. For example, *Should our school have a student newspaper? Explain why.* The answer to the question is their argument: *Our school should have a student newspaper because…* Other questions that can be used to generate arguments include *What is the best…?, What should we do about…?,* or *How can we solve…?*

Focus Trait: Word Choice

Tell students that adjectives can help them show their thoughts and feelings about a topic. Adjectives also can help writers influence readers to think or feel the same way.

Direct students' attention to the descriptive words in the model on p. 26, such as *fantastic, valuable,* and *impressive.* Ask *Do these words suggest that the writer has a positive or negative feeling about student newspapers? What are some words that might be used to express a negative feeling?*

Explain that using too many adjectives, however, can create problems for a writer. Discuss how readers react when a writer uses too many adjectives. Ask students to brainstorm adjectives for a topic, such as pizza. Then have students make up sentences using one, two, and more adjectives about the pizza. How many adjectives does it take before students find the statements unconvincing or suspiciously untrue?

Book Review

Minilesson 15

Supporting Opinions with Evidence

Common Core State Standards: W.6.1a, W.6.1b, W.6.2b

Objective: Develop and support an opinion about a book.

Guiding Question: What are the parts of a book review?

Teach/Model—I Do

Invite students to share types of reviews they may know: movies, cars, restaurants, household items, etc. Point out that reviewers make judgments about quality and give details to support those judgments. Then read aloud handbook p. 28. Point out how the writer stated the title of the book and included quotations and examples from the story to support her opinion.

Guided Practice—We Do

Tell students that a book review makes a judgment about a book. Such judgments should be supported by reasons and evidence from the story. Work together to choose a book all students have read. Guide students to form an opinion about the book. Then have them suggest examples and evidence from the story to support their opinion. Prompt them to come up with strong examples. For example, if they say the plot is interesting, ask *What makes the plot interesting?* List their ideas on the board.

Practice/Apply—You Do

COLLABORATIVE Have pairs work together to choose a book that they have all read and develop an opinion about it. Then have them make a list of examples from the story that support their opinion.

INDEPENDENT Have students choose another book, write an opinion, and choose evidence from the book to support their opinion.

Conference/Evaluate

Work with students to make sure that they have chosen compelling reasons to support their opinions.

Minilesson 16

Drafting a Book Review

Common Core State Standards: W.6.1a, W.6.1b, W.6.4

Objective: Draft a book review.

Guiding Question: How do I plan a book review?

Teach/Model—I Do

Review the model on p. 28. Point out to students that readers have different tastes and that their favorite book might not appeal to readers who prefer different kinds of books or other genres. Explain that this is why good reviewers give reasons for their opinions. Even someone who didn't like the book would still understand the reasons why the writer of the student model liked it because the model gives reasons and examples.

Guided Practice—We Do

 Direct students to the frame on handbook p. 29. Tell them that you will write a book review together. Guide students to choose a book they are all familiar with. Work together to form an opinion of the book. Brainstorm a list of important information for the review: the situation the main character is in, the most interesting elements, and reasons why readers should read the book. Then complete the frame. Have students write in their books as you write on the board.

Practice/Apply—You Do

 COLLABORATIVE Have pairs plan and complete Activity 2. Remind them that they need to provide support for their opinion.

 INDEPENDENT Have students read and follow the directions. Tell them to use their prewriting plan from Lesson 8 or to brainstorm a new plan using Graphic Organizer 7.

Conference/Evaluate

As students draft, have them evaluate their work using the rubric on p. 104.

Book Review

A **book review** is a composition that contains the writer's analysis and opinion of a book or selection.

Parts of a Book Review

- An opening sentence that states the main idea and the author's opinion
- An analysis of setting, character, and plot that supports the author's opinion
- A closing sentence that restates the main idea and the author's recommendation

Opening Sentence Gives main idea and author's opinion	My favorite part of *Science Friction* was the character development. The main character, Amanda, considers herself a "science geek," and she is not pleased about being grouped with "Ms. Perfect," the class clown, and "Mr. Silent" for their class project. We see her detached, organized personality when she uses scientific references to explain things, such as comparing the team members to "inert gases" that don't easily combine. **In addition,** the first-person point of view helps readers really understand what Amanda thinks about her non-science teammates.
Analysis Presents story details that support author's opinion	
Closing Sentence Restates main idea and gives author's recommendation	The best part, however, is how Amanda changes in the story. Even though she isn't happy with her group, she still tries to work with them and compromises when they have different ideas. **In the end,** she discovers that she might have misjudged her teammates a bit and that she could learn some things from them. The "elements" that were reluctant to work together, she learns, end up producing a great science project.
	This story has a realistic main character who learns a valuable lesson. I would recommend it to anyone who likes a good story.

Other Transitions
First
Later
Eventually
After
Next
Following

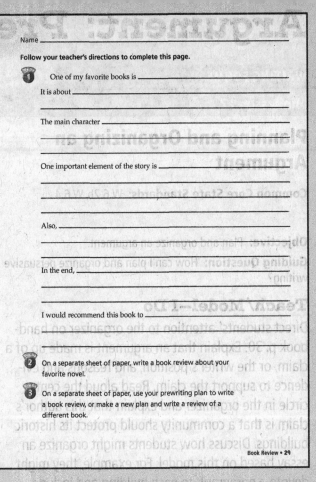

Name _____

Follow your teacher's directions to complete this page.

One of my favorite books is _____

It is about _____

_____

The main character _____

_____

One important element of the story is _____

_____

_____

Also, _____

_____

In the end, _____

_____

I would recommend this book to _____

On a separate sheet of paper, write a book review about your favorite novel.

On a separate sheet of paper, use your prewriting plan to write a book review, or make a new plan and write a review of a different book.

✔ Corrective Feedback

IF . . . students produce a plot summary instead of a review,

THEN . . . remind them that a good reviewer asks *Is this good?* instead of *What happened?* A review is written to help readers judge if they want to read the book. A reviewer who only retells the book's plot will just spoil it for readers. Instead, the reviewer should share an opinion about the book's quality that will help readers decide whether they want to read it themselves.

✏ Focus Trait: Ideas

Remind students that in a book review, writers give evidence from the text to support their opinions. Examples can be paraphrased, or they can be quoted directly from the text and placed in quotation marks.

On the board write *Amanda is a science geek who doesn't care how her room looks.* Ask *Is this a direct or indirect quotation? How do you know?* (Indirect; not Amanda's exact words.)

Then write *"I'd rather spend my time trying to understand the universe than straightening out one little unimportant part of it."* Ask *Is this a direct or indirect quotation? How do you know?* (Direct; quotation marks tell us these are exact words.)

Invite volunteers to paraphrase the direct quotation. Remind students that they can use both paraphrases and direct quotations to support their opinions about a book. Remind them to provide information about where they found direct quotations.

Argument: Prewriting

Minilesson 17 | Minilesson 18

Planning and Organizing an Argument

Common Core State Standards: W.6.2b, W.6.4

Objective: Plan and organize an argument.

Guiding Question: How can I plan and organize persuasive writing?

Teach/Model—I Do

Direct students' attention to the organizer on handbook p. 30. Explain that an argument is made up of a claim, or the writer's position, and reasons and evidence to support the claim. Read aloud the center circle in the organizer and explain that this author's claim is that a community should protect its historic buildings. Discuss how students might organize an essay based on this model. For example, they might devote a paragraph to each building and include details about why the building is important.

Guided Practice—We Do

On the board, draw a web similar to the one on handbook p. 30. Write a claim in the center, such as *the fire department should be better funded by our town.* Work with students to come up with reasons to support the claim, such as *firefighters risk their lives to keep us safe.* Write the reasons in the web on the board.

Practice/Apply—You Do

COLLABORATIVE Have pairs choose another topic related to something they would like to see happen in their town. Have them make a web with the claim in the center and the reasons surrounding it.

INDEPENDENT Have students choose another topic related to preserving something in their town. Have them complete a web related to the topic.

Conference/Evaluate

Circulate and help students choose reasons that are specific and persuasive.

Using Supporting Details

Common Core State Standards: W.6.2b, W.6.4

Objective: Use supporting details to develop a claim.

Guiding Question: What details support my claim?

Teach/Model—I Do

Review p. 30 with students. Mention that the outer bubbles include details about each building explaining why it should be preserved. Remind students that an argument needs plenty of supporting details in the form of reasons and evidence. In turn, the evidence should include facts and examples. Point out that facts and examples can help make an argument more persuasive.

Guided Practice—We Do

 Direct students to Activity 1 on handbook p. 31. Discuss the claim that the community should have a multicultural festival. Work together to come up with reasons why it is important to preserve cultural heritage, such as *some traditions will be lost if we don't practice them* or *we can learn a lot about a culture's history by studying its traditions.* Use students' answers to complete the web. Have students write in their books as you write on the board.

Practice/Apply—You Do

 COLLABORATIVE Have pairs plan and complete Activity 2. Encourage them to provide at least three reasons why museums are important.

 INDEPENDENT Have students read and follow the directions. Tell them to use their prewriting plan from Lesson 9 or to brainstorm a new plan using Graphic Organizer 15.

Conference/Evaluate

As students draft, have them evaluate their work using the rubric on p. 104.

Argument: Prewriting

An **argument** seeks to convince readers to agree with the author's position.

Parts of an Argument

- An introduction that states the topic and the author's personal beliefs about the topic
- A body that uses logical reasoning and factual evidence to support the argument
- A conclusion that sums up the argument

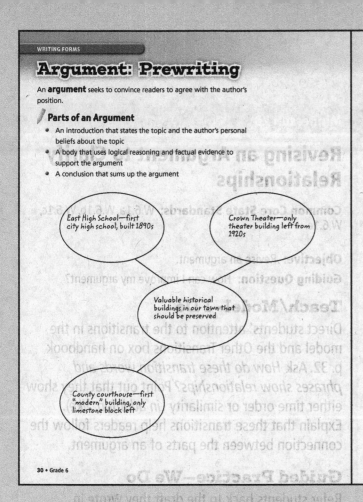

East High School—first city high school, built 1890s

Crown Theater—only theater building left from 1920s

Valuable historical buildings in our town that should be preserved

County courthouse—first "modern" building, only limestone block left

---

Name _____

Follow your teacher's directions to complete this page.

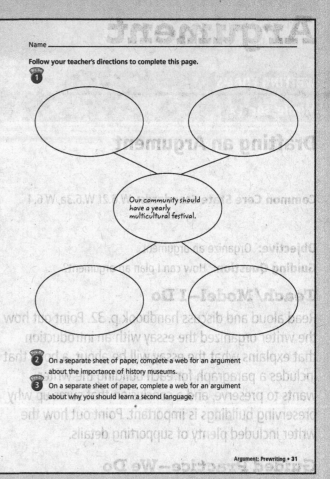

Our community should have a yearly multicultural festival.

 On a separate sheet of paper, complete a web for an argument about the importance of history museums.

 On a separate sheet of paper, complete a web for an argument about why you should learn a second language.

✔ Corrective Feedback

IF . . . students include details or examples that are interesting but do not support their argument,

THEN . . . ask them to explain the relationship between the detail(s) and the point they are trying to prove. They may be able to use some of these details in the introduction to engage readers' interest. However, each piece of supporting evidence in a body paragraph should be related to the claim.

✏ Focus Trait: Ideas

Point out to students that the idea in the central circle of a web can help them decide what to include and what to leave out.

For example, their community has many buildings. However, not all structures have historical significance. Only those connected to history would make good examples.

Ask *What happens if you have too many examples?*

Explain that not all examples are persuasive and that including too many will confuse or bore the reader. One strategy to prevent this is to limit the number of examples by choosing 3 to 5 of the best and writing about those.

Another strategy is to narrow the central idea. For example, a writer might decide to focus on buildings from a certain time period.

Argument

Minilesson 19

Drafting an Argument

Common Core State Standards: W.6.2f, W.6.3a, W.6.4

Objective: Organize an argument.
Guiding Question: How can I plan an argument?

Teach/Model—I Do

Read aloud and discuss handbook p. 32. Point out how the writer organized the essay with an introduction that explains what the essay will be about, a body that includes a paragraph for each building the writer wants to preserve, and a conclusion that sums up why preserving buildings is important. Point out how the writer included plenty of supporting details.

Guided Practice—We Do

 Direct students to the frame on handbook p. 33. Using their prewriting plans from the previous lesson, work together to draft an argument for a community multicultural festival. Guide students to include reasons and facts to support the claim. Have students write in their books as you write on the board.

Practice/Apply—You Do

 COLLABORATIVE Have pairs complete Activity 2 using their prewriting plans from the previous lesson. Encourage them to show why history museums are important..

 INDEPENDENT Have students read and follow the directions. Tell them to use their prewriting plan from Lesson 10 or to brainstorm a new plan using Graphic Organizer 15.

Conference/Evaluate

As students draft, have them evaluate their work using the rubric on p. 104.

- eBook
- WriteSmart
- Interactive Lessons

Minilesson 20

Revising an Argument to Clarify Relationships

Common Core State Standards: W.6.1a, W.6.1b, W.6.1c, W.6.1e.

Objective: Revise an argument.
Guiding Question: How can I improve my argument?

Teach/Model—I Do

Direct students' attention to the transitions in the model and the Other Transitions box on handbook p. 32. Ask *How do these transition words and phrases show relationships?* Point out that they show either time order or similarity (*in addition, like*). Explain that these transitions help readers follow the connection between the parts of an argument.

Guided Practice—We Do

Refer students back to the draft they wrote in Minilesson 19. Work together to read the essay and find places where ideas seem disconnected. Guide students to add transition words and phrases to help connect their sentences and ideas. Guide them to pay particular attention to transition words that help explain the relationships between reasons, such as *It is important to understand how people from other cultures do things **because** some traditions will be lost if we don't. **Additionally**, we can learn a lot from studying traditions.*

Practice/Apply—You Do

COLLABORATIVE Have students work in groups to revise their drafts by adding transition words and phrases.

INDEPENDENT Have students choose another draft they have worked on and revise it to include more transition words.

Conference/Evaluate

Circulate and help students determine where they should add transitions. Remind them that they can use transitions to make their writing easier for the reader to follow.

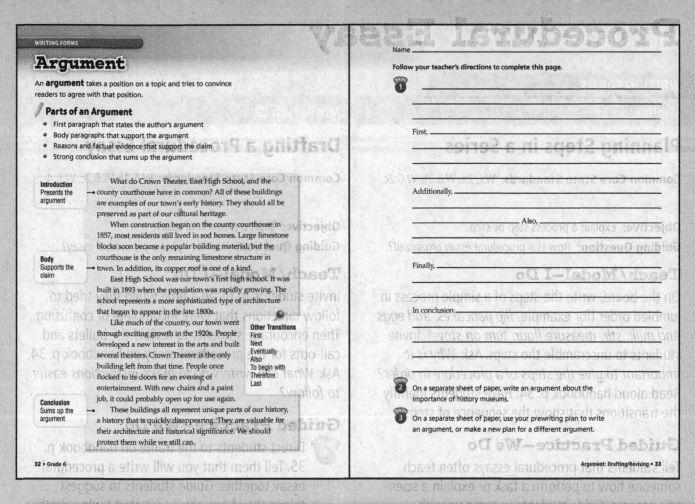

Argument

An **argument** takes a position on a topic and tries to convince readers to agree with that position.

Parts of an Argument
- First paragraph that states the author's argument
- Body paragraphs that support the argument
- Reasons and factual evidence that support the claim
- Strong conclusion that sums up the argument

Introduction
Presents the argument

What do Crown Theater, East High School, and the county courthouse have in common? All of these buildings are examples of our town's early history. They should all be preserved as part of our cultural heritage.

Body
Supports the claim

When construction began on the county courthouse in 1857, most residents still lived in sod homes. Large limestone blocks soon became a popular building material, but the courthouse is the only remaining limestone structure in town. In addition, its copper roof is one of a kind.

East High School was our town's first high school. It was built in 1893 when the population was rapidly growing. The school represents a more sophisticated type of architecture that began to appear in the late 1800s.

Like much of the country, our town went through exciting growth in the 1920s. People developed a new interest in the arts and built several theaters. Crown Theater is the only building left from that time. People once flocked to its doors for an evening of entertainment. With new chairs and a paint job, it could probably open up for use again.

Other Transitions
First
Next
Eventually
Also
To begin with
Therefore
Last

Conclusion
Sums up the argument

These buildings all represent unique parts of our history, a history that is quickly disappearing. They are valuable for their architecture and historical significance. We should protect them while we still can.

Name _____

Follow your teacher's directions to complete this page.

1 _____
_____
_____

First, _____
_____

Additionally, _____
_____

_____ Also, _____
_____

Finally, _____
_____

In conclusion _____
_____

2 On a separate sheet of paper, write an argument about the importance of history museums.

3 On a separate sheet of paper, use your prewriting plan to write an argument, or make a new plan for a different argument.

Corrective Feedback

IF . . . students find it difficult to write a conclusion,

THEN . . . ask them to answer one of these questions: *What is the most important thing your reader should remember? Why should your reader care about your topic?*

Focus Trait: Sentence Fluency

Tell students that most arguments have at least two sides. Writers often include arguments from more than one side of an issue. They might want to cover a complex issue completely or they might want to contrast their opinion with someone else's.

Write this frame on the board: *Some people say _____, but I say _____.* Ask students to suggest ways to complete the frame.

Explain that many transitions can be used to show contrast. Work with students to create a list (*although, on the other hand, in contrast*). Tell students that using transitions that show contrast helps readers distinguish their personal opinion from those of others.

When writers include many examples to prove a point, they can emphasize the strength of their evidence by using transitions that show likeness (*also, in addition, likewise, similarly, in the same way*).

Procedural Essay

Minilesson 21	Minilesson 22

Planning Steps in a Series

Common Core State Standards: W.6.2a, W.6.2b, W.6.2c

Objective: Explain a process step-by-step.

Guiding Question: How is a procedural essay organized?

Teach/Model—I Do

On the board, write the steps of a simple process in jumbled order (for example, *flip pancakes, add eggs and milk, stir, measure flour, turn on stove*). Invite students to unscramble the steps. Ask *Why is it important to give the steps of a procedure in order?* Read aloud handbook p. 34. Have students identify the transitions that show the sequence of steps.

Guided Practice—We Do

Tell students that procedural essays often teach someone how to perform a task or explain a scientific process. Guide students to come up with possible topics for a procedural essay, such as *the digestive process* or *how to make a sandwich*. Work together to choose a process and write the steps of it on the board, such as *Food is ingested, food is mixed with acid in the stomach, food is absorbed by the small intestine*.

Practice/Apply—You Do

COLLABORATIVE Have students work in groups to list the steps of a process. Have them exchange lists, review the steps to see if they are clear and complete, and share any questions they have.

INDEPENDENT Have students work on their own to write a list of steps in a simple process. Have them share their work.

Conference/Evaluate

Have students review their lists to see whether their steps are complete and in order.

Drafting a Procedural Essay

Common Core State Standards: W.6.2a, W.6.2c, W.6.4

Objective: Draft a procedural essay.

Guiding Question: How do I plan a procedural essay?

Teach/Model—I Do

Invite students to recall a time when they tried to follow directions that were incomplete or confusing. Then encourage students to review the bullets and call-outs for the procedural essay on handbook p. 34. Ask *What can writers do to make instructions easier to follow?*

Guided Practice—We Do

 Direct students to the frame on handbook p. 35. Tell them that you will write a procedural essay together. Guide students to suggest things they have always wanted to do, whether practical (play a sport) or whimsical (travel in time). Then brainstorm a list of steps. Consider any safety precautions students would need to take. Finally, complete the frame, asking students to write in their books as you write on the board.

Practice/Apply—You Do

 COLLABORATIVE Have groups plan and complete Activity 2. Remind them that they need to use transitions to show the order in which steps should be completed.

 INDEPENDENT Have students read and follow the directions. Have them use their plans from Lesson 11 or another plan they create using Graphic Organizer 7.

Conference/Evaluate

As students draft, have them evaluate their work using the rubric on p. 104.

 Digital
- eBook
- WriteSmart
- Interactive Lessons

Procedural Essay

A **procedural essay** is a composition that provides a step-by-step process to explain how something is done.

Parts of a Procedural Essay

- An opening that introduces the topic
- Transitions (first, next, last) that present steps in a clear order
- Relevant facts that prove statements are true
- A concluding statement that wraps up the main ideas

Introduction
Identifies topic

Transitions
Steps presented in order

Supporting Facts
Prove statements are true

Concluding Statement

Other Transitions
To begin
Later
Eventually
After
Next
Following

Camping can be a fun and enjoyable way for families to relax and spend time together, but there are several steps you should take before setting off on your adventure. **First,** spend time researching possible campsites. Decide what you want to do, and **then** look for campgrounds that offer those activities. If you enjoy hiking and fishing, search for sites near trails and water.

Second, find and check all of your equipment. Gather everything you will need—cooking utensils, rain gear, sleeping bags—and check to make sure it all works. Set up your tent in the backyard beforehand to make sure there are no holes or tears and that you have all the pieces.

Third, plan your meals. Cooking over a campfire or camp stove is very different from cooking at home. Plan meals that are easy to make as well as nutritious and yummy.

Fourth, always check the weather before setting out. A campout can easily be ruined by a steady rain or a surprise snow storm. If you are camping in the mountains, you should still be prepared for unexpected weather conditions.

Finally, relax and have fun. You are there to get away from the constant busyness of home, so roast those marshmallows, lay back, and enjoy the stars.

34 • Grade 6

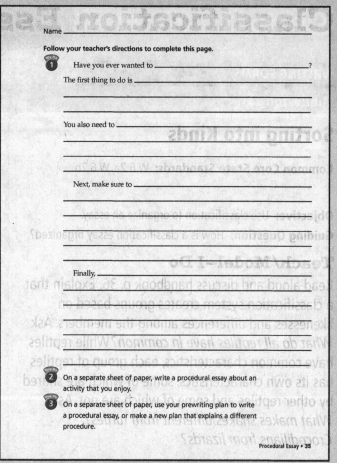

Name _____

Follow your teacher's directions to complete this page.

1. Have you ever wanted to _____?
   The first thing to do is _____
   _____
   _____

   You also need to _____
   _____
   _____

   Next, make sure to _____
   _____
   _____

   Finally, _____
   _____
   _____

2. On a separate sheet of paper, write a procedural essay about an activity that you enjoy.

3. On a separate sheet of paper, use your prewriting plan to write a procedural essay, or make a new plan that explains a different procedure.

Procedural Essay • 35

Corrective Feedback

IF . . . students have difficulty thinking of supporting details,

THEN . . . tell them that people who know how to do something often leave out details that are needed by readers who are not familiar with the process. Writers can capture these critical details by asking *What might go wrong? How will readers know they are following instructions correctly?* For example, a recipe might warn that beating the batter too hard will make pancakes tough.

Focus Trait: Word Choice

Tell students that instructions usually begin with a verb. They are written as imperative sentences; that is, they tell people what to do.

Ask students to find the imperative verbs in the five steps in the model on p. 34 (*spend, find, plan, check, decide, gather*).

Explain that the subject of an imperative verb is not directly stated. However, it is understood to be you.

For example, *Wait here!* is understood to mean *You wait here.*

Ask students to suggest examples of imperative verbs that might be used in procedural essays, such as *turn, place,* or *combine.*

Point out that starting each step in a procedural essay with an imperative verb keeps the focus on the action to be performed.

Classification Essay

Sorting into Kinds

Common Core State Standards: W.6.2a, W.6.2b

Objective: Use classification to organize an essay.

Guiding Question: How is a classification essay organized?

Teach/Model—I Do

Read aloud and discuss handbook p. 36. Explain that a classification system creates groups based on likenesses and differences among the members. Ask *What do all reptiles have in common?* While reptiles have common characteristics, each group of reptiles has its own characteristics, some of which are shared by other reptiles and some of which are not. Ask *What makes snakes different from turtles? Crocodilians from lizards?*

Guided Practice—We Do

Draw a two-column chart on the board with the headings *Group* and *Characteristics*. Write *Buildings* on the board and, beneath it, list several groups, such as *Homes, Offices, Stores, Factories,* and so on. Then elicit characteristics of each group. Ask *What do these groups have in common? How are they different from each other?*

Practice/Apply—You Do

COLLABORATIVE Have students work in pairs to make a similar 2-column chart for a topic like *dogs* or *music.*

INDEPENDENT Have students choose another topic and create a chart on their own.

Conference/Evaluate

Have students check the accuracy of their criteria by asking whether a member of one group could also belong to another group.

Drafting a Classification Essay

Common Core State Standards: W.6.2a, W.6.2b

Objective: Draft a classification essay.

Guiding Question: How do I plan a classification essay?

Teach/Model—I Do

Review handbook p. 36. Read aloud the first paragraph and remind students that a classification essay needs a brief summary toward the beginning that names the parts of the topic. Point out that the summary in the model makes it clear that this essay will be about kinds of reptiles.

Guided Practice—We Do

 Direct students to the frame on handbook p. 37. Tell them that together you will write a classification essay. Work with students to choose a topic, which could be a science topic they have studied or another topic of interest, such as popular musicians. Then have students explore different classifications. Discuss whether the categories are complete and exclusive (in other words, a member of one group cannot also belong to another.) Then complete the frame together. Have students write in their books as you write on the board.

Practice/Apply—You Do

 COLLABORATIVE Have pairs plan and complete Activity 2. Remind them to introduce the topic, include a brief summary, discuss each group, and wrap things up with a conclusion.

 INDEPENDENT Have students read and follow the directions. Tell them to use their prewriting plan from Lesson 12 or to brainstorm a new plan using Graphic Organizer 15.

Conference/Evaluate

As students draft, have them evaluate their work using the rubric on p. 104.

Digital
• eBook
• WriteSmart
• Interactive Lessons

Classification Essay

A **classification essay** explains a topic by discussing its parts.

Parts of a Classification Essay
- An introduction that presents the topic
- A brief summary that names the parts of the topic
- An explanation of each part
- A conclusion that wraps up and restates the main points

Introduction Presents the topic	Reptiles are a large group of animals that have been around for millions of years. They are vertebrates, have scaly skin, and usually lay eggs. They **also** are cold-blooded. There are four groups of reptiles alive today: snakes and lizards, turtles and tortoises, crocodilians, and the tuatara.
Brief Summary Names the main parts of the topic	
	Snakes and lizards make up the largest group of reptiles with over 5,700 different species. Some lizards and all snakes are legless. Legless lizards are different from snakes in that lizards have eardrums and eyelids and snakes do not.
Body Paragraphs Explain each part	Turtles and tortoises are the **second** largest group of reptiles with over 200 species. They have shells protecting their bodies. Most of the shells are hard, but some are soft and leathery.
	Crocodiles, alligators, caimans, and gavials are the **next** group, called crocodilians. There are 23 species, and they are the oldest and most advanced reptiles. They are more closely related to birds than to other reptiles.
	The smallest group is the tuatara, which look like lizards. Tuatara live in New Zealand even though their closest relatives went extinct millions of years ago.
Conclusion Wraps up the main ideas and facts	Reptiles may not be cute and cuddly, but they are an interesting and diverse group of animals that have been around for a long time.

Other Transitions
First
Later
Eventually
After
Following
Then
For example
Finally

Name _____

Follow your teacher's directions to complete this page.

1 _____ are _____

_____

_____

The first _____

_____

The second _____

_____

The next _____

_____

_____ In addition _____

_____

In conclusion, _____

2 On a separate sheet of paper, write a classification essay about your favorite activity or hobby.

3 On a separate sheet of paper, use your prewriting plan to write a classification essay, or make a new plan that explores a different topic.

✓ Corrective Feedback

IF . . . students are having difficulty developing categories,

THEN . . . encourage them to think of as many examples of the topic as they can. For example, if the topic is cats, they might list *house cats, jaguars, lions, cheetahs,* and *leopards.* Then have students organize their list into larger, more inclusive groups. For example, they might classify cats into domestic cats and jungle cats.

Focus Trait: Voice

Tell students that classification essays can be humorous. For example, a student might write an essay classifying pets into three categories: *Boring, Most Popular, and Feared by Mothers Everywhere.* In this case, the writer's tone would probably be informal with lots of humorous exaggeration.

Most classification essays, however, are like the model. The writer is objective, and the essay focuses on facts instead of personal experiences or feelings.

(For example, the writer does not exclaim, "I hate snakes" or "I am terrified of alligators.") In addition, the language is mostly neutral. (For example, the writer avoids describing snakes with adjectives like *scary* or *fascinating.*)

This formal voice puts the focus on the content. The writer takes on the role of an expert who helps readers understand a complicated topic by breaking it down into parts.

Definition Essay

Minilesson 25

Using More Than One Definition

Common Core State Standards: W.6.2a, W.6.2b

Objective: Use definitions to organize an essay.

Guiding Question: How is a definition essay organized?

Teach/Model—I Do

Read aloud and discuss handbook p. 38. Ask *In how many ways does the author define* courage? Point out that, in addition to the dictionary definition and the writer's personal definition, in this essay *courage* is defined by example—the actions of the writer's family members. Help students recognize that by defining the word in more than one way the writer helps readers better understand just what the writer means by the word *courage.*

Guided Practice—We Do

Remind students that, when Americans fought for independence, Patriots supported independence and Tories were loyal to Britain. Ask *How would a Patriot have defined the term* American Revolution? *How would a Tory have defined it?* Brainstorm a list of other words and terms that people might define differently, such as *competition, freedom,* or *health.* If students have difficulty developing ideas, tell them that abstract ideas often make good topics for a definition essay.

Practice/Apply—You Do

COLLABORATIVE Ask pairs to choose a term from the list and complete this frame: *Some people think that _____ means _____. To us it means _____.*

INDEPENDENT Have students choose another topic and complete this frame: *Some people think that _____ means _____, but to me it means_____.*

Conference/Evaluate

Have students evaluate whether their definitions go beyond basic dictionary definitions of a term.

Minilesson 26

Drafting a Definition Essay

Common Core State Standards: W.6.2a, W.6.2b

Objective: Draft a definition essay.

Guiding Question: How do I plan a definition essay?

Teach/Model—I Do

Remind students that the same word can mean different things to different people. Review handbook p. 38, discussing the call-outs and helping students understand how the writer builds a personal definition of courage. Show how this could be extended by adding other examples from personal experience.

Guided Practice—We Do

 Direct students to the frame on handbook p. 39. Tell them that together you will write a definition essay. Work with students to choose a topic, such as *generosity.* Discuss the dictionary meaning of the term, identify a common belief or misunderstanding about the topic, and brainstorm examples that illustrate its meaning. (Example: *Some people think being generous is only about money. But one can also have generosity of spirit.*) Then complete the frame together. Have students write in their books as you write on the board.

Practice/Apply—You Do

 COLLABORATIVE Have pairs plan and complete Activity 2. Remind them that one of the most effective ways to begin a definition essay is by contrasting what the writer thinks with what other people think.

 INDEPENDENT Have students read and follow the directions. Tell them to use their prewriting plan from Lesson 13 or to brainstorm a new plan using Graphic Organizer 7.

Conference/Evaluate

As students draft, have them evaluate their work using the rubric on p. 104.

Definition Essay

A **definition essay** explains the meaning of a word or phrase.

Parts of a Definition Essay

- An introduction that defines the word or phrase
- Examples and details that support and explain the definition
- Details that tell what the word means to the writer
- A summary that wraps up the definition and examples

Introduction Defines the word	The dictionary defines "courage" as the ability to face danger or difficulty, but I think there is a lot more to it than that. Real courage requires an inner strength that most people don't know they have until they have to use it. I'm lucky because four of the most courageous people I know are in my own family.
Examples and Details Support the definition	I'll **start** with my great-grandparents who lived in Atlanta, Georgia, during the 1960s. They sacrificed their livelihoods and many friendships when they joined the civil rights movement. They showed great courage by speaking out for what they knew was right even though their opinion was unpopular at the time.
	My **next** example is my aunt, who shows courage when she runs into burning buildings to rescue people from fires. She has been a firefighter for ten years and says, "It's just part of the job." But I know she is very courageous. Not many people would risk their own lives to save the lives of complete strangers.
Details Tell what the word means to the writer	**Finally,** my little brother is the very definition of courage. He was born with a disease that will keep him in a wheelchair his entire life. He has faced five surgeries, will never know what it is like to kick a soccer ball, and yet always has a smile on his face and a kind word for everyone he meets.
Summary Wraps up the definition and examples	These are the people I think of when I think of courage. They are brave, principled, and hopeful. They are my heroes.

Transitions
First
To begin with
Later
Eventually
After
Following
Then
For example
Such as

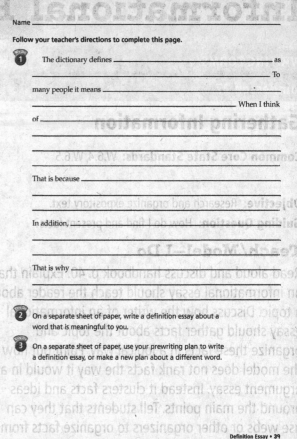

Name _____

Follow your teacher's directions to complete this page.

1 The dictionary defines _____ as
_____ To
many people it means _____
_____ When I think
of _____
_____
_____

That is because _____
_____

In addition, _____
_____

That is why _____

2 On a separate sheet of paper, write a definition essay about a word that is meaningful to you.

3 On a separate sheet of paper, use your prewriting plan to write a definition essay, or make a new plan about a different word.

Corrective Feedback

IF . . . students have trouble writing definitions for their essays,

THEN . . . challenge them to define common terms such as *happy*, *best*, or *nice*. Help students understand that people tend to define such terms according to their own lives and experiences. Remind students that a definition essay is simply a way to state one's own definition of a common term that is understood in different ways.

Focus Trait: Organization

Guide students to see that a good way to organize a definition essay is by comparison and contrast. They might begin by describing an idea in detail. They could then compare it to something similar and, finally, contrast it with something else.

Have students look at the model on p. 38 and see how they might reorganize the material using comparison and contrast. For example, while the aunt shows courage by helping others, the brother shows personal courage and leads by example.

Next, point out that a definition essay also could be organized in order of importance. Work with students to reorganize the examples in the model on p. 38 in this way, arranging them from least important to most important.

Informational Essay: Prewriting

Minilesson 27

Gathering Information

Common Core State Standards: W.6.4, W.6.5

Objective: Research and organize expository text.
Guiding Question: How do I find and present facts?

Teach/Model—I Do

Read aloud and discuss handbook p. 40. Explain that an informational essay should teach the reader about a topic. Discuss how the writer of an informational essay should gather facts about the topic and organize these facts in a logical way. Point out how the model does not rank facts the way it would in an argument essay. Instead it clusters facts and ideas around the main points. Tell students that they can use webs or other organizers to organize facts from their research.

Guided Practice—We Do

Work with students to think of a list of animals, such as *walrus*, *jaguar*, *whale*, and *condor* and write them on the board. Have students choose one as a topic. Point out that there are many topics that a writer would investigate when writing about one of these creatures. Then have students arrange the terms *life cycle*, *diet*, *defenses*, and *habitat* around the animal name, as in the model. With students, use print and/or electronic media to find information about two subtopics. Help students put that information in the appropriate places on the board.

Practice/Apply—You Do

COLLABORATIVE Have pairs choose another topic from the list. Have them use what they know to fill out a web about the topic and then find information about one subtopic.

INDEPENDENT Have individuals choose a different topic and repeat the above activity.

Conference/Evaluate

Circulate and help students find information about their chosen topic.

Minilesson 28

Planning an Informational Essay

Common Core State Standards: W.6.4, W.6.5

Objective: Organize an informational essay.
Guiding Question: How do I plan my informational essay?

Teach/Model—I Do

Review handbook p. 40. Read aloud the model and point out the abbreviated way in which the author fills in the information. Explain that the web does not include full sentences or paragraphs; it concentrates on getting down the main points and information. Note that, when writers refer to textbooks or other sources for information, they do not copy information verbatim into their webs; instead, they write brief notes in their own words.

Guided Practice—We Do

 Direct students to Activity 1 on handbook p. 41. Elicit names of musical instruments and write them on the board. Work with students to name the four main types of instruments: *string, woodwind, brass,* and *percussion.* Guide students to find details about each type of instrument. Then work together to complete the organizer using details students find. Have students write in their books as you write on the board.

Practice/Apply—You Do

 COLLABORATIVE Have pairs plan and complete Activity 2. Direct them to use print and/or electronic media for their research and to include plenty of details in their organizer.

 INDEPENDENT Have students read and follow the directions. Tell them to use their prewriting plan from Lesson 14 or to brainstorm a new plan using a web.

Conference/Evaluate

As students draft, have them evaluate their work using the rubric on p. 104.

Informational Essay: Prewriting

An **informational essay** uses facts and details to tell readers about a topic.

Parts of an Informational Essay

- An introduction that presents a clearly defined topic
- A body that gives main ideas with supporting details
- A conclusion that summarizes the ideas presented

Topic: Incan Gods

Inti—sun god, was supreme. Nourished the earth and crops.

Virocacha—made people from clay. Made sun, moon and stars.

Incas believed in many different gods that were connected to their daily lives.

Illapa—weather god

Zaramama—goddess of grain and corn

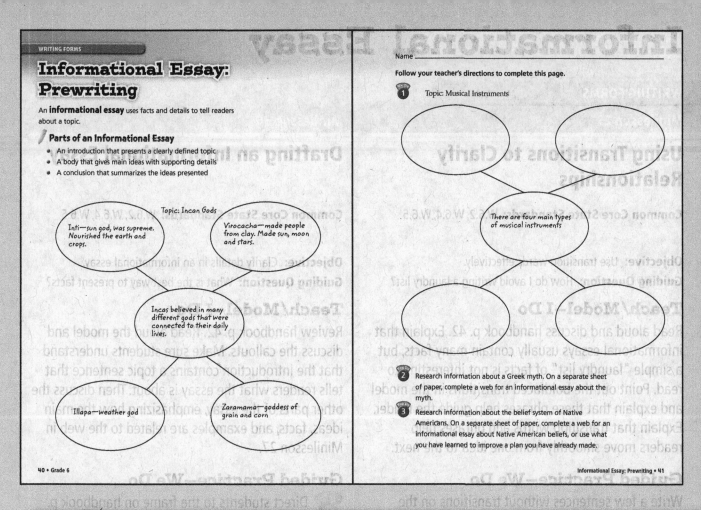

Follow your teacher's directions to complete this page.

1 Topic: Musical Instruments

There are four main types of musical instruments

2 Research information about a Greek myth. On a separate sheet of paper, complete a web for an informational essay about the myth.

3 Research information about the belief system of Native Americans. On a separate sheet of paper, complete a web for an informational essay about Native American beliefs, or use what you have learned to improve a plan you have already made.

 ## Corrective Feedback

IF . . . students are having a hard time finding details to fill out their webs,

THEN . . . encourage them to use textbooks, reference books, the Internet, or other classroom resources to find information about their topic. They can also ask themselves questions like *What do I know? What do I want to know? What have I learned?*

Focus Trait: Ideas

Tell students that they can use the Internet to research ideas for informational essays. If students are using class notes or their own knowledge to plan an informational essay, they might want to use the Internet to double-check their facts. A search engine will help them find websites with information about their topic.

Remind students that if they are researching a topic solely with Internet sources, they need to be conscious of where they find their information.

Some online sources, such as those from governments or universities, are usually reliable. Newspaper websites and websites associated with zoos or museums are probably also reliable. Anyone can put a site on the web, so some information does not always come from recognized experts or is not as carefully fact-checked. Tell students to think critically as they look for information. (See also *Using the Internet* on handbook p. 94.)

Informational Essay

Minilesson 29

Using Transitions to Clarify Relationships

Common Core State Standards: W.6.2, W.6.4, W.6.5

Objective: Use transition words effectively.
Guiding Question: How do I avoid writing a laundry list?

Teach/Model—I Do

Read aloud and discuss handbook p. 42. Explain that informational essays usually contain many facts, but a simple "laundry list" of facts is not interesting to read. Point out the boldfaced transitions in the model and explain that these phrases help guide the reader. Explain that transition words and phrases help readers move smoothly from one idea to the next.

Guided Practice—We Do

Write a few sentences without transitions on the board, such as *Violins are string instruments. The musician plays one by drawing the bow across the strings. The hair on the bow rubs on the strings. The strings vibrate. The wood base of the instrument amplifies the sound.* Work with students to rewrite the paragraph, adding transition words. For example, *The hair on the bow rubs on the strings. This causes the strings to vibrate.*

Practice/Apply—You Do

COLLABORATIVE Write another set of sentences on the board, such as *Trumpet players blow into their instruments through closed lips. Their lips vibrate against the mouthpiece. The air in the trumpet vibrates and makes a sound.* Have pairs rewrite by adding transitions.

INDEPENDENT Have students choose an old draft and rewrite it by adding transition words.

Conference/Evaluate

Circulate and help students write transitions. Explain that these can be time order, cause and effect, or another kind of transition word.

Minilesson 30

Drafting an Informational Essay

Common Core State Standards: W.6.2, W.6.4, W.6.5

Objective: Clarify details in an informational essay.
Guiding Question: What is the best way to present facts?

Teach/Model—I Do

Review handbook p. 42. Read aloud the model and discuss the callouts. Make sure students understand that the introduction contains a topic sentence that tells readers what the essay is about. Then discuss the other parts of the essay, emphasizing how the main ideas, facts, and examples are related to the web in Minilesson 27.

Guided Practice—We Do

 Direct students to the frame on handbook p. 43. Return to the plan made during Minilesson 28. Then work together to complete the frame, turning ideas in the organizer into full sentences. Start by writing an introductory sentence, such as *There are four main kinds of musical instruments.* Work together to write details about each kind of instrument to complete the frame. Have students write in their books as you write on the board.

Practice/Apply—You Do

 COLLABORATIVE Have pairs plan and complete Activity 2. Tell students they can use their plan from the previous lesson to draft an essay. Remind them to use transitions.

 INDEPENDENT Have students read and follow the directions. Tell them to use their plan from the previous lesson or to brainstorm a new plan using Graphic Organizer 15.

Conference/Evaluate

As students draft, have them evaluate their work using the rubric on p. 104.

Informational Essay

An **informational essay** is a composition in which the writer gives information about a topic, using supporting facts and details.

Parts of an Informational Essay

- An introduction that states the topic
- Body paragraphs with main ideas and supporting details
- Supporting facts and examples that are paraphrased or quoted from a resource
- Precise vocabulary related to the topic
- A conclusion that summarizes the essay's ideas

Introduction States the topic	The Inca people, who lived in Peru in the fifteenth and sixteenth centuries, believed in many gods. Their gods were connected to the Inca's daily life.
Body Contains main ideas and supporting details	The sun god, Inti, was the supreme god of the Incas. Everyone had to worship him. **The reason that** he was important was the Inca's belief that he nourished the earth and its crops with his rays. The most important Inca festival, Inti Raymi, celebrated his power. During the festival, the emperor offered gold and silver to Inti.
Facts and examples	**Another** important Inca god was Viracocha. He made humans out of clay and gave them language. He also made the sun, moon, and stars and placed them in the sky. **In addition,** the Inca people worshipped at least twenty other gods. The Incas believed many of the gods controlled the weather and the growth of crops. These things were very important to the Inca way of life. Zaramama, for example, was the goddess of grain and corn. Illapa was a weather god.
Conclusion Summarizes ideas	**In conclusion,** the Incas worshipped many gods because they wanted to understand the world. By having gods that controlled different parts of their everyday world, they hoped that their worship would improve their lives.

Other Transitions
To begin with
Also
Second
Additionally
Finally
In summary
To sum up

Name _____

Follow your teacher's directions to complete this page.

1 _____
_____
_____
_____

(Main idea and details) _____
_____
_____
_____

(Main idea and details) _____
_____
_____
_____

In conclusion, _____
_____

2 On a separate sheet of paper, use your plan to write an informational essay about a Greek myth.

3 On a separate sheet of paper, use your prewriting plan to write an informational essay, or plan and write an informational essay about a topic of your choice.

Corrective Feedback

IF . . . students are having a hard time coming up with appropriate transition words,

THEN . . . have them tell a partner the relationship between two ideas. Then have the students refer to a list of transition words and find the one that best expresses that relationship. This relationship might be sequence of events, cause and effect, or spatial, for example.

Focus Trait: Voice

Remind students that most informational writing is formal, rather than informal or chatty as a narrative might be. Point out how the model on p. 42 uses formal language to present facts. Informational writing also does not include opinions.

Write a few sentences on the board, such as:

Brass instruments are really cool. You change the pitch on a trombone by pulling on the slide thingie.

Woodwind instruments don't have to be made of wood. I've seen flutes made of metal.

Have students rewrite the sentences to sound more formal. For example:

Brass musicians change pitch in different ways. They change the pitch on a trombone by using the slide.

Not all woodwind instruments are made of wood. Many flutes are made of metal.

Compare-Contrast Essay

Using a Venn Diagram

Common Core State Standards: W.6.2a, W.6.4, W.6.5

Objective: Use a Venn diagram to organize ideas.
Guiding Question: How can I organize my ideas?

Teach/Model—I Do

With students, read aloud and discuss handbook p. 44. Explain that to *compare* is to show similarities, and to *contrast* is to show differences. Mention that a Venn diagram can help writers organize their ideas. Draw a Venn diagram on the board. Label the circles *president* and *governor*. Elicit from students contrasting facts about the two jobs (*the president leads the country; the governor leads the state*) and write them in the outer parts of the diagram. Point out that the middle section shows facts that are true for both jobs (*both are elected*). Model how to look up facts from a source, such as an encyclopedia.

Guided Practice—We Do

Help students think of topics to compare and contrast, such as *mammals* and *reptiles*. Draw a Venn diagram on the board. Together, use two sources to find facts about each topic. Guide students to determine where facts should be written in the diagram. Continue until there are three facts in each section of the diagram.

Practice/Apply—You Do

COLLABORATIVE Have groups of students use two sources to find facts and complete a Venn diagram about traveling by airplane and by train. Have groups discuss their ideas.

INDEPENDENT Have students work independently to repeat the exercise and complete a Venn diagram with facts about two movies they have seen.

Conference/Evaluate

Circulate and guide students to identify similarities and differences.

Drafting a Compare-Contrast Essay

Common Core State Standard: W.6.2a

Objective: Write an essay that compares and contrasts.
Guiding Question: How can I explain how two things are different and the same?

Teach/Model—I Do

Have students review the definition and Parts of a Compare-Contrast Essay. Read aloud the model, pointing out that it is organized by differences and then similarities. Point out the boldfaced transitions. Go over the list in the Other Transitions box.

Guided Practice—We Do

 Direct students to the frame on handbook p. 45. Draw a Venn diagram on the board, and guide students to suggest similarities and differences. If necessary, let students use reference sources to find information, or suggest these categories of differences: *speed*, *power source*, and *safety*. Write sentences together to complete the frame, starting with differences. Have students write in their books as you write on the board.

Practice/Apply—You Do

 COLLABORATIVE Have small groups plan and complete Activity 2. Remind them to write a clear topic sentence for each paragraph. Have groups share what they have written.

 INDEPENDENT Have students read the directions. Tell them to use their prewriting plan from Lesson 16 or to brainstorm a new plan using Graphic Organizer 14.

Conference/Evaluate

As students draft, circulate and help them choose similarities and differences. Evaluate using the rubric on p. 104.

Digital
- eBook
- WriteSmart
- Interactive Lessons

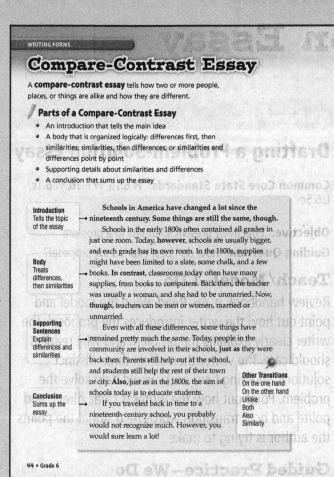

Compare-Contrast Essay

A **compare-contrast essay** tells how two or more people, places, or things are alike and how they are different.

Parts of a Compare-Contrast Essay

- An introduction that tells the main idea
- A body that is organized logically: differences first, then similarities; similarities, then differences; or similarities and differences point by point
- Supporting details about similarities and differences
- A conclusion that sums up the essay

Introduction
Tells the topic of the essay

Body
Treats differences, then similarities

Supporting Sentences
Explain differences and similarities

Conclusion
Sums up the essay

Schools in America have changed a lot since the nineteenth century. Some things are still the same, though.

Schools in the early 1800s often contained all grades in just one room. Today, **however,** schools are usually bigger, and each grade has its own room. In the 1800s, supplies might have been limited to a slate, some chalk, and a few books. **In contrast,** classrooms today often have many supplies, from books to computers. Back then, the teacher was usually a woman, and she had to be unmarried. Now, **though,** teachers can be men or women, married or unmarried.

Even with all these differences, some things have remained pretty much the same. Today, people in the community are involved in their schools, **just as** they were back then. Parents still help out at the school, and students still help the rest of their town or city. **Also,** just as in the 1800s, the aim of schools today is to educate students.

If you traveled back in time to a nineteenth-century school, you probably would not recognize much. However, you would sure learn a lot!

Other Transitions
On the one hand
On the other hand
Unlike
Both
Also
Similarly

44 • Grade 6

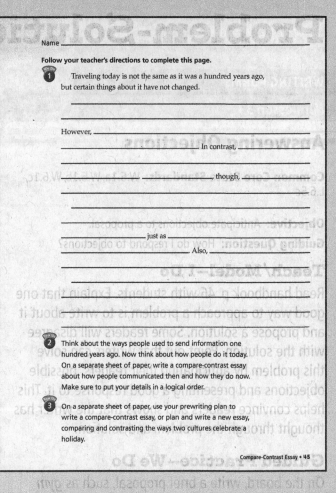

Name _____

Follow your teacher's directions to complete this page.

1 Traveling today is not the same as it was a hundred years ago, but certain things about it have not changed.

_____
_____
_____

However, _____
_____
_____, In contrast,
_____
_____
_____, though, _____
_____
_____
_____, just as _____
_____
_____, Also,
_____
_____

2 Think about the ways people used to send information one hundred years ago. Now think about how people do it today. On a separate sheet of paper, write a compare-contrast essay about how people communicated then and how they do now. Make sure to put your details in a logical order.

3 On a separate sheet of paper, use your prewriting plan to write a compare-contrast essay, or plan and write a new essay, comparing and contrasting the ways two cultures celebrate a holiday.

Compare-Contrast Essay • 45

Corrective Feedback

IF . . . students are having trouble identifying similarities and differences,

THEN . . . have them first list the characteristics of one of their subjects and then do the same for the other. Tell them to compare their lists and find similarities. Have students put the similarities into the center of a Venn diagram. Have them then find pairs of differences, which they should list on either side of the diagram. Tell students not to use items on one list that are unrelated to items on the other list.

Focus Trait: Ideas

Tell students that, when they choose a topic for an essay, they should be sure not to choose something too broad or too narrow. A broad topic will have too much information. A narrow topic won't have enough.

Write a few examples of topics for a compare-contrast essay that are too broad or too narrow, such as:

Grandma's red sedan

boats

spacecraft

Discuss how the broad and narrow topics are hard to write about. Have students identify whether each topic is too broad or too narrow *(too narrow; too broad; too broad)* and then work together to find good alternatives for a topic for a compare-contrast essay. For example:

a modern sedan and a Ford Model T

sailboats and motorboats

the space shuttle and the Mars rover

Problem-Solution Essay

Minilesson 33

Answering Objections

Common Core State Standards: W.6.1a, W.6.1b, W.6.1c, L.6.5c

Objective: Anticipate objections to a proposal.

Guiding Question: How do I respond to objections?

Teach/Model—I Do

Read handbook p. 46 with students. Explain that one good way to approach a problem is to write about it and propose a solution. Some readers will disagree with the solution. Point out that writers can solve this problem by anticipating their readers' possible objections and presenting a good response to it. This helps convince readers and shows that the writer has thought through the problem and solution.

Guided Practice—We Do

On the board, write a brief proposal, such as *gym class should be mandatory.* Work with students to come up with a few reasons to support the proposal, such as *everyone needs exercise* or *it's good to get a break from schoolwork.* Guide students to come up with a few objections, such as *Kids should be able to choose their own activities instead of being forced into gym class.* Then work together to answer the objection. For example, *Gym class is the only physical activity most students get.*

Practice/Apply—You Do

COLLABORATIVE Have students come up with another proposal, such as *everyone should take a music class.* Have groups work together to come up with possible objections and write responses.

INDEPENDENT Have students choose another proposal, such as *our school should have a student newspaper.* Then have them write a few possible objections and responses to those objections.

Conference/Evaluate

Have students evaluate their responses to see if they effectively answer possible objections.

Minilesson 34

Drafting a Problem-Solution Essay

Common Core State Standards: W.6.1a, W.6.1b, W.6.1c, L.6.5c

Objective: Effectively present solutions to a problem.

Guiding Question: How do I best express my proposal?

Teach/Model—I Do

Review handbook p. 46. Read aloud the model and point out how the writer introduces the proposal. The writer clearly explains the problem and why readers should care. The writer then offers three distinct solutions, showing how each would help solve the problem. Point out how the writer is clear, direct, and polite and how transition words help signal the points the author is trying to make.

Guided Practice—We Do

 Direct students to the frame on handbook p. 47. Work together to write about a problem, such as *our school needs more computers* and a few possible solutions, such as *We can solve this problem by holding a fundraiser to raise money for computers.* Ask students to rank the solutions, keeping in mind just how useful and practical each solution might be. Remind them to anticipate objections and address them. Fill in the frame to complete the activity. Have students write in their books as you write on the board.

Practice/Apply—You Do

 COLLABORATIVE Have groups plan and complete Activity 2. Have groups share their work.

 INDEPENDENT Have students read and follow the directions. Tell them to use their prewriting plan from Lesson 17 or to brainstorm a new plan using Graphic Organizer 7.

Conference/Evaluate

As students draft, have them evaluate their work using the rubric on p. 104.

 Digital
- eBook
- WriteSmart
- Interactive Lessons

Problem-Solution Essay

A **problem-solution essay** is a composition that explains a problem and suggests possible solutions.

Parts of a Problem-Solution Essay

- An introduction with details and examples that make the problem clear to the reader
- Reasonable solutions that are each explained by details
- Transition words that link examples and signal each solution to the problem
- A conclusion that restates the author's position

Introduction
Explains the problem in detail

Transition Words
Link examples and signal each solution

Details
Support reasonable solutions to the problem

Conclusion
Restates the author's arguments

Community Park is a great place that offers activities for everyone, but an increase in traffic has made this jewel of our town dangerous to reach. There is no room for parking, so most people walk to Community Park from their homes or from parking lots several blocks away. Fast cars and dark streets make this walk risky, especially for families with young children. Fortunately, a few simple changes can help walkers stay safe.

To begin with, lower the speed limit to 20 mph on the streets downtown. Slower-moving drivers can pay better attention to pedestrians and can stop faster. **In addition,** install stoplights at the crosswalks. This will discourage people from jaywalking in the middle of the street and force cars to stop for pedestrians.

Finally, add more street lamps. There are many evening events at Community Park, like summer concerts and baseball games, but there is little lighting after dark. Additional street lamps will not only make it easier for cars to see pedestrians but will make the park safer in general.

These measures will go a long way in making Community Park a fun and safe place for our entire community.

Other Transitions
First, second, third
Then
After
Next
Following
First of all
For example

46 • Grade 6

Name _____

Follow your teacher's directions to complete this page.

One problem that affects our class is _____
_____
_____
_____

We can solve this problem by _____

First of all, _____

For example, _____
_____
In addition, _____

Last of all, _____
_____

On a separate sheet of paper, write a problem-solution essay about a problem at your school.

On a separate sheet of paper, use your prewriting plan to write a problem-solution essay, or make a new plan that solves a different problem.

Problem-Solution Essay • 47

Corrective Feedback

IF . . . students are having a hard time coming up with responses to objections,

THEN . . . have them role play with a friend. Student 1 offers a problem and a solution. Student 2 responds, objecting to the proposed solution. Student 1 then responds to Student 2's objection(s), working this response into the essay.

Focus Trait: Word Choice

Tell students that, when identifying a problem and proposing solutions, they want to earn the respect and trust of their reader. This means using clear and polite language. If a reader can see that the writer has put time and thought into crafting a good essay and choosing exact words, then the reader is more likely to trust the writer's opinion.

It is also important to be constructive when identifying a problem. It is not useful to write about

a problem that is expressed as "art class is stupid and boring." Point out that this is not going to be seen as a valid or well thought-out problem/solution essay. Ask students to brainstorm ways they could express their dissatisfaction while being polite, thoughtful, and constructive.

Grade 6 • **47**

Cause-Effect Essay

Minilesson 35	**Minilesson 36**

Identifying Causes and Effects

Common Core State Standard: W.6.2a

Objective: Identify causes and their effects.

Guiding Question: How can I figure out which events are causes and which are effects?

Teach/Model—I Do

With students, read and discuss the information and model on handbook p. 48. Reread the first two sentences. Explain that these state a cause (a Greek army attacked Troy) and an effect (this brought on the Trojan War). Then explain that there are other effects in the paragraph. Write *Both sides grew weary of the fighting* and *Odysseus devised a plan.* Explain that the first is an effect but also a cause of the second. Help students understand that effects answer the question *What happened as a result?* Explain that some causes have more than one effect and some effects, more than one cause.

Guided Practice—We Do

Tell students to suppose they want to write a cause-effect paragraph about the Civil War. Have them suggest causes for the war, and then ask them for effects of the war. If necessary, they can look for ideas in reference books or online sources. Write their suggestions on the board.

Practice/Apply—You Do

COLLABORATIVE Write a number of topics on the board, such as *going west by covered wagon* and *the American Revolution.* Have small groups write a cause and an effect for one of the topics. Encourage them to use multiple sources for help.

INDEPENDENT Have students write one cause and one effect for the other topic, using reference sources.

Conference/Evaluate

Circulate and ask students to explain the relationships between the causes and effects they found.

Drafting a Cause-Effect Essay

Common Core State Standard: W.6.2a

Objective: Write a strong cause-effect essay.

Guiding Question: How can I state a cause and explain its effects?

Teach/Model—I Do

Have students review the definition and Parts of a Cause-Effect Essay on handbook p. 48. Reread the model, pointing out various cause-and-effect relationships as well as the boldfaced transitions that help show causes, effects, and time order. Go over the list in the Other Transitions box.

Guided Practice—We Do

 Direct students to the frame on handbook p. 49. Point out the topic sentence and transitions. Explain that the topic sentence tells an event that was the cause of many others. Guide students to suggest details explaining the effects of the event, such as *Katrina caused a storm surge; storm surge caused breaks in levees; 80 percent of New Orleans flooded.* You may want to let students use newspaper or magazine articles to find effects. With students, develop sentences to complete the frame, giving the final effect last. Have students write in their books as you write on the board.

Practice/Apply—You Do

 COLLABORATIVE Have small groups plan and complete Activity 2. Tell them to complete the topic sentence with details showing that the Boston Tea Party caused many events. Then have them finish the paragraph with effects of the Tea Party. Have groups share their work.

 INDEPENDENT Have students read and follow the directions.

Conference/Evaluate

Make sure students are coming up with effects of the events listed and not causes.

Cause-Effect Essay

A **cause-effect essay** tells about something that happened and the person, object, or event that made it happen.

Parts of a Cause-Effect Essay

- A introduction that states a cause, an effect, or both
- Precise details that tell the causes, or why things happened
- Details that tell effects, or what happened
- Transition words or phrases that connect ideas
- A conclusion that describes the final effect

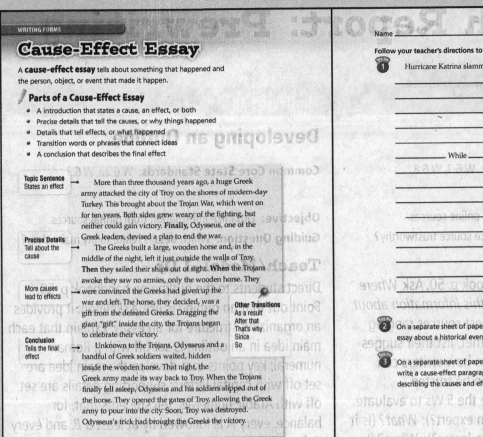

Topic Sentence States an effect

More than three thousand years ago, a huge Greek army attacked the city of Troy on the shores of modern-day Turkey. This brought about the Trojan War, which went on for ten years. Both sides grew weary of the fighting, but neither could gain victory. **Finally,** Odysseus, one of the Greek leaders, devised a plan to end the war.

Precise Details Tell about the cause

The Greeks built a large, wooden horse and, in the middle of the night, left it just outside the walls of Troy. **Then** they sailed their ships out of sight. **When the Trojans** awoke they saw no armies, only the wooden horse. They

More causes lead to effects

were convinced the Greeks had given up the war and left. The horse, they decided, was a gift from the defeated Greeks. Dragging the giant "gift" inside the city, the Trojans began to celebrate their victory.

Other Transitions
As a result
After that
That's why
Since
So

Conclusion Tells the final effect

Unknown to the Trojans, Odysseus and a handful of Greek soldiers waited, hidden inside the wooden horse. That night, the Greek army made its way back to Troy. When the Trojans finally fell asleep, Odysseus and his soldiers slipped out of the horse. They opened the gates of Troy, allowing the Greek army to pour into the city. Soon, Troy was destroyed. Odysseus's trick had brought the Greeks the victory.

Name _____

Follow your teacher's directions to complete this page.

 1 Hurricane Katrina slammed into New Orleans in August of 2005.

_____

_____ Then _____

_____

_____ However, _____

_____

_____ While

_____

_____ Because of _____

_____

_____

_____

2 On a separate sheet of paper, plan and write a cause-effect essay about a historical event you learned about in school.

3 On a separate sheet of paper, use your prewriting plan to write a cause-effect paragraph, or plan and write a paragraph describing the causes and effects of a historical event.

Corrective Feedback

IF . . . students are unable to show how causes lead to effects,

THEN . . . encourage them to make a list of cause-and-effect transitions, such as *because* and *as a result*. They can use these words to make cause-and-effect relationships clear. Additionally, encourage them to organize their writing in time order.

Focus Trait: Sentence Fluency

Explain to students that a variety of sentence lengths and beginnings can make their writing more interesting to read and easier to follow. On the board, write

People who went west by covered wagon helped change our country. People who traveled this way opened up the West.

Have students suggest ways in which the sentences can be varied to make them more interesting to read.

Examples:

People who went west by covered wagon helped change our nation. By their pioneering actions, they opened up the West.

Point out that the introductory phrase *By their pioneering actions* is a transition that makes the sentence flow smoothly.

Research Report: Prewriting

Minilesson 37

Researching Online

Common Core State Standards: W.6.7, W.6.8

Objective: Assess the credibility of online sources.

Guiding Question: Is this reference source trustworthy?

Teach/Model—I Do

Read aloud and discuss handbook p. 50. Ask *Where do you think the writer found this information about blue whales?* As students suggest sources ranging from encyclopedias to the Internet, list their suggestions on the board. Then discuss how writers can determine whether a source can be trusted. Emphasize that writers can use the 5 Ws to evaluate sources: *Who?* (Is the author an expert?); *What?* (Is it an in-depth report or something lesser?); *When?* (Is the information up to date?); *Where?* (Is the source sponsored by a university or respected organization?); *Why?* (Did the author write to give information or to persuade?) Then, using the 5 Ws, show how to rank students' suggested sources according to trustworthiness, from 1 (the most trustworthy) to 5 (the least).

Guided Practice—We Do

Tell students that an Internet search for "giant squid" will yield information from many sources, from government agencies to an elementary school class project. Work with students to list a number of possible sources on the board. Help students use the 5Ws to rank the sources for trustworthiness.

Practice/Apply—You Do

COLLABORATIVE Have groups work together to make a list of possible sources for a report on sharks and rank them by trustworthiness.

INDEPENDENT Have students choose a marine mammal to be a topic for a report and write a list of possible sources for the report. Have them rank the sources for trustworthiness.

Conference/Evaluate

Ask students to justify their *1* ranking for sources.

Minilesson 38

Developing an Outline

Common Core State Standards: W.6.2a, W.6.7

Objective: Organize information from digital sources.

Guiding Question: Which details relate to my main ideas?

Teach/Model—I Do

Direct students to the outline on handbook p. 50. Point out that an outline is like a skeleton: it provides an organizing structure for an essay. Explain that each main idea in an outline is set off with a Roman numeral; key points that develop the main idea are set off with capital letters; supporting details are set off with Arabic numerals. Tell students that, for balance, every *A* is followed by at least a *B*, and every *1*, by at least a *2*. There may be more items (C, D, E etc. or 3, 4, 5), but there should be at least two.

Guided Practice—We Do

 Direct students to Activity 1 on handbook p. 51. Work with students to research information about manatees and what is being done to protect them. Together, write an outline about manatees. Have students write in their books as you write on the board.

Practice/Apply—You Do

 COLLABORATIVE Have groups complete Activity 2. Point out that each main idea (habitat, appearance, and reason it is endangered) will get a Roman numeral.

 INDEPENDENT Have students read and follow the directions. Tell them to use their prewriting plan from Lesson 19 or to brainstorm a new plan using an outline.

Conference/Evaluate

As students draft, have them evaluate their work using the rubric on p. 104.

Digital
• eBook
• WriteSmart
• Interactive Lessons

Research Report: Prewriting

A **research report** uses facts taken from multiple sources to closely analyze an idea or topic.

Parts of a Research Report

- A thesis statement that introduces a clear topic
- A body with main ideas and supporting details
- Facts and examples gathered from research
- A conclusion that summarizes the ideas presented

Topic: Blue Whales

```
I. Background
    A. largest mammal
        1. 80-100 ft
        2. 100-200 tons
    B. found in every ocean
    C. eat krill

II. Endangered Species
    A. overhunted
        1. hundreds of thousands before 1900
        2. one whale provided 120 barrels of oil
        3. 29,000 killed in 1931
        4. nearly extinct by 1960s
    B. efforts to save whales
        1. hunting banned in 1966
        2. 1970 listed as endangered

III. Conclusion
    A. only between 5,000 and 12,000 remain
    B. conservation efforts can hopefully save them
```

Name _____

Follow your teacher's directions to complete this page.

 Topic: Manatee

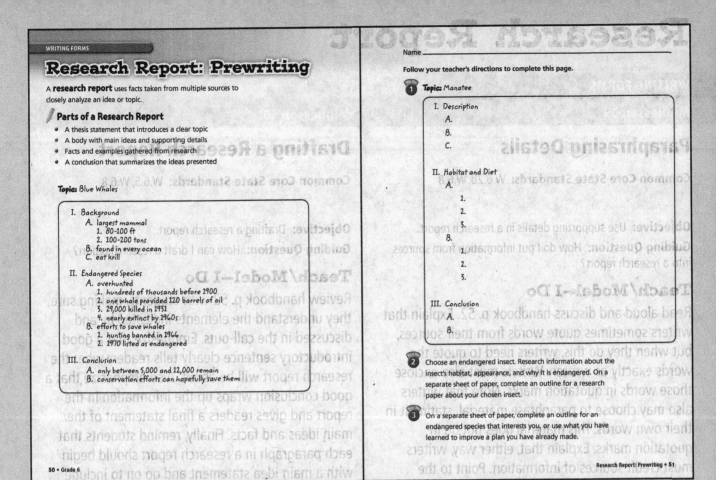

```
I. Description
    A.
    B.
    C.

II. Habitat and Diet
    A.
        1.
        2.
        3.
    B.
        1.
        2.
        3.

III. Conclusion
    A.
    B.
```

2 Choose an endangered insect. Research information about the insect's habitat, appearance, and why it is endangered. On a separate sheet of paper, complete an outline for a research paper about your chosen insect.

3 On a separate sheet of paper, complete an outline for an endangered species that interests you, or use what you have learned to improve a plan you have already made.

Research Report: Prewriting • 51

 ## Corrective Feedback

IF . . . students find it difficult to develop an outline,

THEN . . . suggest that they create a reverse outline. First, have them list all of the details they can. Then have them sort the details into categories. For example, a list including pizza, spaghetti, tacos, calzones, and enchiladas might be sorted into *Italian Food* and *Mexican Food* or *Foods to Eat with Fingers* and *Foods to Eat with Knife, Fork, and Spoon*. Finally, have students number the groups they want to include in their report in the order they plan to write about them.

Focus Trait: Organization

Tell students that some reports use headings to help the reader understand how information is organized. These boldfaced headings tell the reader what topic that section of the report will focus on.

Have students turn to the outline on handbook p. 50. Point out that *I. Background* can be written as the section heading **Introduction** in the draft. **Endangered Species** will be the heading of the second section of the draft. Explain that a section can contain more than one paragraph as long as

they all relate to the heading. Tell students that headings are particularly useful when writing a longer, more in-depth research report.

Ask students to suggest other subject headings for the outline on blue whales, such as *Evolution* and *Life Cycle*. Remind students that adding more subject headings often means expanding the focus of the research paper and that they should make sure to only add headings that relate to their specific topic.

Research Report

Minilesson 39

Paraphrasing Details

Common Core State Standards: W.6.2b, W.6.8

Objective: Use supporting details in a research report.

Guiding Question: How do I put information from sources into a research report?

Teach/Model—I Do

Read aloud and discuss handbook p. 52. Explain that writers sometimes quote words from their sources, but when they do this, writers need to quote the words exactly as written. Writers must also enclose those words in quotation marks. Note that writers also may choose to paraphrase material, stating it in their own words. This material does not go in quotation marks. Explain that, either way, writers must credit sources of information. Point to the parenthetical citations in the model.

Guided Practice—We Do

Choose a textbook or other book in the classroom and copy a quotation from the book onto the board. Then work with students to paraphrase the quote. Remind them to use their own words and not to copy directly from the source.

Practice/Apply—You Do

COLLABORATIVE Have groups look up information in a textbook, other book, or the Internet on great white sharks. Have them choose a passage from their source and work together to paraphrase the passage.

INDEPENDENT Have students look up information about octopuses and paraphrase a passage from their source.

Conference/Evaluate

Circulate and make sure students are using their own words when paraphrasing.

Minilesson 40

Drafting a Research Report

Common Core State Standards: W.6.5, W.6.8

Objective: Drafting a research report.

Guiding Question: How can I draft a research report?

Teach/Model—I Do

Review handbook p. 52 with students, making sure they understand the elements indicated by and discussed in the call-outs. Emphasize that a good introductory sentence clearly tells readers what the research report will be about. Also emphasize that a good conclusion wraps up the information in the report and gives readers a final statement of the main ideas and facts. Finally, remind students that each paragraph in a research report should begin with a main idea statement and go on to include facts and details that support the main idea.

Guided Practice—We Do

 Direct students to the frame on handbook p. 53, working with them to gather information about manatees. Help students form main idea statements for two paragraphs. Guide them to complete the activity. Have students write in their books as you write on the board.

Practice/Apply—You Do

 COLLABORATIVE Have groups complete Activity 2. Remind them to use quotation marks when they use the exact words of a source.

 INDEPENDENT Have students read and follow the directions. Tell them to use their prewriting plan from the previous lesson or to brainstorm a new plan.

Conference/Evaluate

As students draft, have them evaluate their work using the rubric on p. 104.

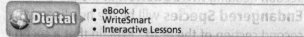

Digital
- eBook
- WriteSmart
- Interactive Lessons

Research Report

A **research report** is a composition in which the writer closely examines a topic or idea. A research report uses factual information gathered and paraphrased from several sources.

Parts of a Research Report

- An introduction or thesis statement stating the topic
- Body paragraphs with main ideas and supporting details
- Facts and examples as supporting details
- A conclusion that sums up the main points

Introduction Clearly states the topic	**Introduction**
	The blue whale is thought to be the largest mammal on Earth. It may not hold that title for long. **It is endangered and may soon disappear.**
Body Paragraphs Use details to support each main idea	Blue whales are about 80 to 100 feet long and weigh from 100 to 200 tons. They are found in every ocean on Earth, and they eat mostly krill, which are tiny animals like shrimp (Hale 25). They are not a threat to humans, but humans are a terrible threat to them.
	Endangered Species
Facts and Examples Support the main ideas	Before the 1900s, there were hundreds of thousands of blue whales in the world's oceans. **However,** they were prized by whale hunters because of their great size. A single blue whale could provide up to 120 barrels of oil. In one year, 1931, over 29,000 whales were killed. By the 1960s, the blue whale was nearly extinct (Richards 100–101).
Information Source Tells where paraphrased information was found	In 1966, the International Whaling Commission banned hunting of blue whales. **Soon after,** in 1970, the United States Fish and Wildlife Service listed the blue whale as endangered.
Conclusion Sums up the report	**Although** many of the blue whales are gone forever, there are still a few thousand left (Jenkins 90). With efforts by wildlife conservation groups, it is possible that these enormous creatures will be saved.

Other Transitions
To begin with
Meanwhile
Until
But
For instance
In conclusion

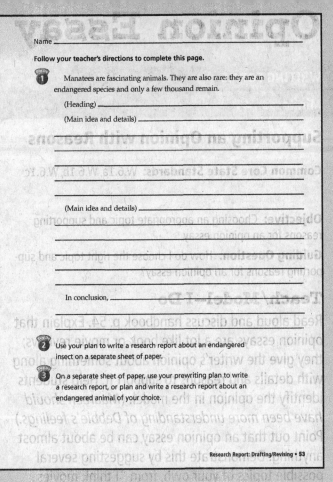

OPINION ESSAY

Name _____

Follow your teacher's directions to complete this page.

1 Manatees are fascinating animals. They are also rare: they are an endangered species and only a few thousand remain.

(Heading) _____

(Main idea and details) _____

_____

_____

_____

(Main idea and details) _____

_____

_____

In conclusion, _____

2 Use your plan to write a research report about an endangered insect on a separate sheet of paper.

3 On a separate sheet of paper, use your prewriting plan to write a research report, or plan and write a research report about an endangered animal of your choice.

Corrective Feedback

IF . . . an attempt to paraphrase is still too close to the original because students changed only a few words,

THEN . . . suggest that students write notes about the information in their own words and then paraphrase. Explain that plagiarism means copying words exactly, and that plagiarism is like stealing the words an author wrote. When writers paraphrase, they restate information accurately using their own words and phrases. Have students find another passage and guide them to take notes before they paraphrase.

Focus Trait: Ideas

One way to identify the most important ideas in a source is to make a copy of the information and underline key words as you read.

Write an example on the board, such as, *Blue whales are about 80 to 100 feet long and weigh from 100 to 200 tons.*

Ask students to identify the key words and phrases: *blue whales; 80 to 100 feet long; 100 to 200 tons.*

Ask volunteers to restate that information, encouraging them to change the order. For example, *Blue whales are immense. They may weigh up to 200 tons and grow up to 100 feet long.*

Have students compare the paraphrase to the original. Ask *Is the important information included? Does the paraphrase sound too much like the original?* Have students work with a partner to paraphrase three sentences from a source they used.

Opinion Essay

Minilesson 41

Supporting an Opinion with Reasons

Common Core State Standards: W.6.1a, W.6.1b, W.6.1c

Objective: Choosing an appropriate topic and supporting reasons for an opinion essay.

Guiding Question: How do I choose the right topic and supporting reasons for an opinion essay?

Teach/Model—I Do

Read aloud and discuss handbook p. 54. Explain that opinion essays are a lot like book or movie reviews; they give the writer's opinion about something along with details and reasons to support it. Help students identify the opinion in the model. (*Maureen should have been more understanding of Debbie's feelings.*) Point out that an opinion essay can be about almost anything. Demonstrate this by suggesting several possible topics of your own, from "I think movies should be less violent" to "Rainy days are better than sunny days."

Guided Practice—We Do

Emphasize that an opinion essay needs strong supporting reasons as well as a solid opinion statement. With students, brainstorm and list on the board possible topics, such as "Lunch time should be longer" or "Students should do more volunteer work." Help students make a list of possible supporting reasons for each topic.

Practice/Apply—You Do

COLLABORATIVE Have groups choose one of the topics from the board and then expand and strengthen the list of reasons.

INDEPENDENT Have students choose a different topic from the board and expand the list of reasons on their own.

Conference/Evaluate

Have students evaluate their lists to see that their reasons are relevant and persuasive.

Minilesson 42

Drafting an Opinion Essay

Common Core State Standards: W.6.1a, W.6.1b, W.6.1c

Objective: Choose the best structure for an opinion essay.

Guiding Question: How do I draft my opinion essay?

Teach/Model—I Do

Review handbook p. 54. Read aloud the model and point out the ways in which the writer supports her opinion. She explains the scenario in the book and expresses a clear opinion about the character's actions. Point out the three criticisms the author makes about Maureen's behavior. Note that the author draws an overall conclusion about Maureen's character, which was supported by the specific criticisms. Point out that this structure (statement—reasons—conclusion) is often effective for opinion essays.

Guided Practice—We Do

 Direct students to the frame on handbook p. 55. Tell them that together you will write an opinion essay about why being in a school play is beneficial to students. Guide students to suggest specific examples; then fill in the frame together. Have students write in their books as you write on the board.

Practice/Apply—You Do

 COLLABORATIVE Have groups plan and complete Activity 2. Groups should decide together on an opinion to use for the essay.

INDEPENDENT Have students read and follow the directions. Tell them to use their prewriting plan from Lesson 21 or to brainstorm a new plan using Graphic Organizer 7.

Conference/Evaluate

As students draft, have them evaluate their work using the rubric on p. 104.

 Digital
- eBook
- WriteSmart
- Interactive Lessons

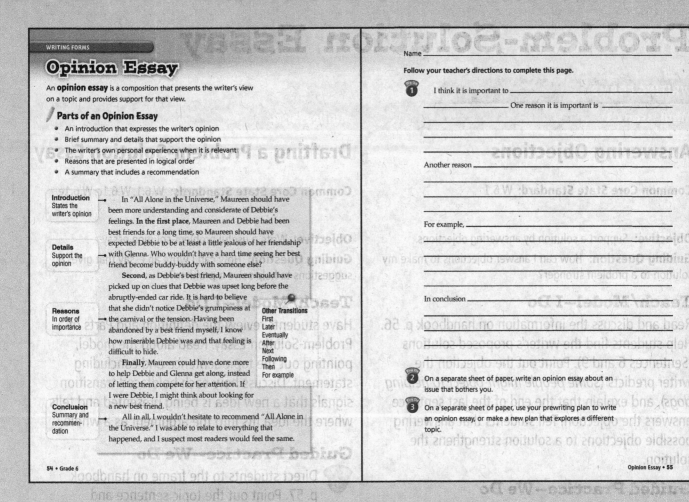

Opinion Essay

An **opinion essay** is a composition that presents the writer's view on a topic and provides support for that view.

Parts of an Opinion Essay

- An introduction that expresses the writer's opinion
- Brief summary and details that support the opinion
- The writer's own personal experience when it is relevant
- Reasons that are presented in logical order
- A summary that includes a recommendation

Introduction
States the writer's opinion

In "All Alone in the Universe," Maureen should have been more understanding and considerate of Debbie's feelings. **In the first place**, Maureen and Debbie had been best friends for a long time, so Maureen should have expected Debbie to be at least a little jealous of her friendship with Glenna. Who wouldn't have a hard time seeing her best friend become buddy-buddy with someone else?

Details
Support the opinion

Second, as Debbie's best friend, Maureen should have picked up on clues that Debbie was upset long before the abruptly-ended car ride. It is hard to believe that she didn't notice Debbie's grumpiness at the carnival or the tension. Having been abandoned by a best friend myself, I know how miserable Debbie was and that feeling is difficult to hide.

Reasons
In order of importance

Other Transitions
First
Later
Eventually
After
Next
Following
Then
For example

Finally, Maureen could have done more to help Debbie and Glenna get along, instead of letting them compete for her attention. If I were Debbie, I might think about looking for a new best friend.

Conclusion
Summary and recommendation

All in all, I wouldn't hesitate to recommend "All Alone in the Universe." I was able to relate to everything that happened, and I suspect most readers would feel the same.

54 • Grade 6

Name _____

Follow your teacher's directions to complete this page.

1. I think it is important to _____
_____ One reason it is important is _____
_____
_____
_____

Another reason _____
_____
_____

For example, _____
_____
_____

In conclusion _____
_____
_____
_____

2. On a separate sheet of paper, write an opinion essay about an issue that bothers you.

3. On a separate sheet of paper, use your prewriting plan to write an opinion essay, or make a new plan that explores a different topic.

Opinion Essay • 55

Corrective Feedback

IF . . . students are struggling with finding reasons to support their opinions,

THEN . . . have them make a list of characteristics of their topic. For example, a student writing about the opinion *Dogs make better pets than cats* could list several descriptions of dogs, such as *furry, cuddly, friendly, obedient, do tricks.* Then, the student could circle the descriptions that they think make dogs better than cats and write those details as reasons, such as *Dogs can be taught tricks* or *Dogs are friendlier.*

Focus Trait: Voice

Writers use a different voice depending on their audience. An opinion essay might be written in a formal or informal voice. Remind students that an informal voice is often used in writing to peers but that a formal voice is often used when writing to strangers. Tell students that, when writing formally, they should remember to be polite and respectful.

Ask students to name an activity that they enjoy. Then say *I think that _____ is stupid!* Ask students

how they feel about that response, eliciting that they probably feel defensive, angry, or insulted. Point out that a writer should try not to make readers feel that way. How could a negative opinion of the activity have been expressed in a more polite way? Write student suggestions on the board and evaluate the effects of the possible alternatives. Then have students practice phrasing other opinion statements in a respectful manner.

Problem-Solution Essay

Minilesson 43

Answering Objections

Common Core State Standard: W.6.1

Objective: Support a solution by answering objections.

Guiding Question: How can I answer objections to make my solution to a problem stronger?

Teach/Model—I Do

Read and discuss the information on handbook p. 56. Help students find the writer's proposed solutions (Sentences 6 and 9). Point out the objection the writer predicts (*some people might object to helping dogs*), and explain that the end of the last sentence answers the objection. Tell students that answering possible objections to a solution strengthens the solution.

Guided Practice—We Do

On the board, write *Drivers go too fast near the school, so we should lower the speed limit.* Have students think of possible objections to the solution, such as *Kids aren't in the street in the middle of the day* and *School is closed in the summer.* Ask them to suggest some answers to the objections, such as *Some kids walk home for lunch* and *Summer school is in session.* Write their suggestions on the board.

Practice/Apply—You Do

COLLABORATIVE On the board, write two new solutions, such as *We should put solar panels on our school to save energy* and *Our town should start a community garden to grow food for those in need.* Have partners think of an objection to one of the solutions and write an answer to it.

INDEPENDENT Have students write a possible objection to the second solution. Then have them answer the objection.

Conference/Evaluate

Encourage any students having trouble thinking of possible objections to brainstorm with partners who do not share their point of view.

Minilesson 44

Drafting a Problem-Solution Essay

Common Core State Standards: W.6.1, W.6.1c, W.6.1e

Objective: Write a useful problem-solution essay.

Guiding Question: How can I write an essay that gives suggestions to help solve a problem?

Teach/Model—I Do

Have students review the definition and Parts of a Problem-Solution Essay. Read aloud the model, pointing out the topic sentence and concluding statement. Discuss how each boldfaced transition signals that a new idea is being presented and tells where the idea fits into the argument as a whole.

Guided Practice—We Do

 Direct students to the frame on handbook p. 57. Point out the topic sentence and transitions. Guide students to identify the problem and suggest possible solutions, such as creating a skating park. List ideas on the board, and guide students to use them to suggest sentences to complete the frame. Include details that explain the solution and a concluding statement. Have students write in their books as you write on the board.

Practice/Apply—You Do

 COLLABORATIVE Have partners plan and complete Activity 2. Tell them to complete the topic sentence with their idea of a problem in their school. Have partners share and discuss what they have written.

 INDEPENDENT Have students read the directions. Tell them to use their prewriting plan from Lesson 22 or to brainstorm a new plan using Graphic Organizer 7.

Conference/Evaluate

As students draft, circulate and make sure they are presenting a realistic solution to the problem.

- eBook
- WriteSmart
- Interactive Lessons

Problem-Solution Essay

A **problem-solution essay** states a problem and suggests at least one solution.

Parts of a Problem-Solution Essay

- A topic sentence that states the problem
- Details and examples that make the problem clear
- One or more reasonable solutions, with details that explain them
- Transition words that link examples and signal solutions
- A concluding statement that sums up the writer's opinion

Topic Sentence
States the problem

Our community has a lot of dog lovers, but there is no place for them to take their pets without bothering the people who don't like dogs. I have two ideas to fix this problem.

Examples
Make the problem clear

Our local park is a beautiful place, but dog owners don't always pick up after their pets. **In addition,** owners often let their dogs off the leash, and this bothers and even scares other people. I can offer two possible ways to solve the problem. The **first** is to enforce the dog laws. There are already signs about keeping dogs on a leash and picking up after them. Ticketing people who don't obey those rules would help. My **second** idea is to create a dogs-only area. There is a section of the park that is rarely used. With a fence, it could work really well as a meeting place for dogs and their owners. It would be a place where pets could run and play off-leash.

Possible Solutions

Details
Explain solutions

Other Transitions
To begin with
Also
Not only
In closing
Therefore

Concluding Statement
Sums up the writer's opinion

In conclusion, while some people might object to helping dogs, dogs are very important to many people, and dogs certainly deserve a place to have fun.

56 • Grade 6

Name _____

Follow your teacher's directions to complete this page.

A lot of kids in our community want to skateboard and inline skate, but there really isn't any place to do either activity. _____

_____

_____

_____ In addition, _____

_____

_____

_____ First, _____

_____

_____

_____

Second, _____

_____

_____

_____

In conclusion, _____

_____

2. On a separate sheet of paper, plan and write a problem-solution essay about a problem in your school. Include at least one possible solution.

3. On a separate sheet of paper, use your prewriting plan to write a problem-solution essay, or plan and write an essay about a problem in your community and a possible solution.

Problem-Solution Essay • 57

✓ Corrective Feedback

IF . . . students are unable to come up with at least one solution to the problem,

THEN . . . have them break down the problem into parts and think of ways to solve each part of it. They can use an idea-support map like Graphic Organizer 7 and write each part of the problem in a separate box. Then they can jot down possible solutions and details that explain them.

Focus Trait: Word Choice

Tell students that one way to keep their writing interesting is to avoid repeating words and to replace vague, general words with more specific nouns and adjectives. Write a few sentences with dull or vague words on the board.

Some of us get bored during break. Some people started the day camp so that kids have a place to do stuff and meet people.

Work with students to revise these sentences. For example:

Some kids feel bored during summer vacation. As a solution, a group of local college students started a day camp so that elementary and middle school students have a place to play fun games, learn exciting sports, and meet new friends.

Grade 6 • **57**

Persuasive Letter

Minilesson 45

Supporting a Goal with Reasons

Common Core State Standard: W.6.1b

Objective: Use reasons to support a goal.

Guiding Question: How can I get readers to agree with my goal?

Teach/Model—I Do

With students, read and discuss handbook p. 58. Explain that the second sentence states the writer's goal. In the body of the letter, the writer gives three strong reasons why the reader should agree with her opinion. Point out each reason and explain how it supports the writer's goal. The writer also cites the mayor, a person of respect and authority who agrees with her. Explain that citing an authoritative source can be an effective way to convince readers. Other authoritative sources include resources found through research. Remind students that they must credit their sources.

Guided Practice—We Do

Tell students to suppose they want to write a persuasive letter to convince students to vote in school elections. Guide students to suggest reasons, such as *Elected students will make decisions that affect you.* List the reasons on the board. Then help students to find reasons that could be strengthened by reference to an authoritative source, such as the principal.

Practice/Apply—You Do

COLLABORATIVE Write a number of goals on the board, such as *get my friend to run for class president* and *persuade my principal to let students vote on the school lunch menu.* Have small groups write reasons to support one of the goals.

INDEPENDENT Have students write reasons that support the other goal.

Conference/Evaluate

If students have trouble finding reasons, then encourage them to think about why the goal is important to them.

Minilesson 46

Drafting a Persuasive Letter

Common Core State Standards: W.6.1, W.6.1c, W.6.1d

Objective: Write a convincing persuasive letter.

Guiding Question: How can I convince someone to take a specific action?

Teach/Model—I Do

With students, review handbook p. 58. Go over business letter format. Explain that the boldfaced transitions show relationships among ideas, and that *further* and *to sum up* are more formal language than would be found in a friendly letter.

Guided Practice—We Do

 Direct students to the frame on handbook p. 59. Tell them you will write a letter persuading the school board to extend the school year to eleven months. Complete the greeting. Guide students to clearly state the goal and write it as the topic sentence. Then have them suggest reasons to support the goal (examples: *Students would learn more; Students would be better prepared for college and the workforce*). Together, complete the frame. Have students write in their books as you write on the board.

Practice/Apply—You Do

 COLLABORATIVE Have small groups plan and complete Activity 2. Tell them to start with a topic sentence that states the goal and continue with strong reasons to support their opinion. Have groups share and discuss what they have written.

 INDEPENDENT Have students read the directions. They can use their plan from Lesson 23 or brainstorm a new plan using Graphic Organizer 7.

Conference/Evaluate

As students draft, circulate and help them choose reasons that will help achieve their goal.

Persuasive Letter

In a **persuasive letter,** the writer tries to persuade the reader to think or do something.

Parts of a Persuasive Letter

- Often, business letter format: heading, inside address, greeting, body, closing, and signature
- A goal, or opinion, with a specific action for the reader to take
- Reasons that support the writer's goal
- Language that is more formal than in a friendly letter

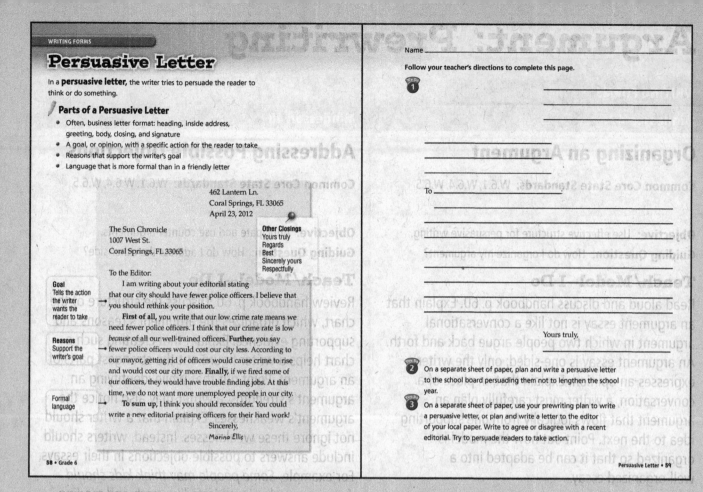

462 Lantern Ln.
Coral Springs, FL 33065
April 23, 2012

The Sun Chronicle
1007 West St.
Coral Springs, FL 33065

Other Closings
Yours truly
Regards
Best
Sincerely yours
Respectfully

To the Editor:

Goal Tells the action the writer wants the reader to take

I am writing about your editorial stating that our city should have fewer police officers. I believe that you should rethink your position.

First of all, you write that our low crime rate means we need fewer police officers. I think that our crime rate is low *because* of all our well-trained officers. **Further,** you say

Reasons Support the writer's goal

fewer police officers would cost our city less. According to our mayor, getting rid of officers would cause crime to rise and would cost our city more. **Finally,** if we fired some of our officers, they would have trouble finding jobs. At this time, we do not want more unemployed people in our city.

Formal language

To sum up, I think you should reconsider. You could write a new editorial praising officers for their hard work!

Sincerely,
Marina Ellis

58 • Grade 6

Name _____

Follow your teacher's directions to complete this page.

① _____
_____
_____

_____
_____

To _____
_____
_____

_____

Yours truly,

② On a separate sheet of paper, plan and write a persuasive letter to the school board persuading them not to lengthen the school year.

③ On a separate sheet of paper, use your prewriting plan to write a persuasive letter, or plan and write a letter to the editor of your local paper. Write to agree or disagree with a recent editorial. Try to persuade readers to take action.

Persuasive Letter • 59

Corrective Feedback

IF . . . students are unable to come up with convincing reasons,

THEN . . . have them make sure their goal is realistic. It would be hard to get readers to agree with a goal like *Sixth-graders should always get free pizza anywhere in town.* It would be easier to get support for a more specific, reasonable goal, such as *Sixth-graders with straight-A report cards should each get one free slice of pizza at Omega Pizza.* Encourage students to think about how they can present their goal so that readers will be receptive to their ideas.

Focus Trait: Ideas

Explain to students that the reasons they use to persuade can be either logical or emotional. On the board, write this logical reason for requiring that dogs wear ID tags:

ID tags allow shelters, rescue groups, and individuals to alert a dog's owner quickly.

Point out that this reason appeals to logic by giving a fact. Then elicit a reason that supports the goal by appealing to emotions.

Example: *Think about how upset you would be if your dog were lost.*

Point out to students that they should use mostly logical reasons when they are trying to persuade.

Argument: Prewriting

Organizing an Argument

Common Core State Standards: W.6.1, W.6.4, W.6.5

Objective: Use effective structure for persuasive writing.
Guiding Question: How do I organize my argument?

Teach/Model—I Do

Read aloud and discuss handbook p. 60. Explain that an argument essay is not like a conversational argument in which two people argue back and forth. An argument essay is one-sided; only the writer expresses an opinion. Explain that, in place of a conversation, a writer must carefully plan an argument that flows logically from one supporting idea to the next. Point out how the model is organized so that it can be adapted into a well-organized essay.

Guided Practice—We Do

 Direct students to Activity 1 on handbook p. 61. Together, plan an argument that supports a claim about technology, such as *schools should use digital textbooks*. Work together to come up with reasons and evidence to support this claim. For example, *Digital textbooks are easy to search. You can type a word into a search box instead of flipping through the index.* Have students write three reasons and three pieces of evidence to support each reason. Guide them to organize the ideas in the three-column chart in their books as you write on the board.

Practice/Apply—You Do

 COLLABORATIVE For Activity 2, have pairs support a claim about the use of cell phones in your school.

 INDEPENDENT Have students choose a new topic and write reasons and evidence to support their claim.

Conference/Evaluate

Circulate and make sure students are using facts and examples to support their claims and not just opinions.

Addressing Possible Objections

Common Core State Standards: W.6.1, W.6.4, W.6.5

Objective: Anticipate and use counter-arguments.
Guiding Question: How do I address the other side?

Teach/Model—I Do

Review handbook p. 60. Discuss the structure of the chart, which organizes the argument's reasons and supporting evidence. Explain that creating such a chart helps a writer figure out the strongest parts of an argument. Point out that while identifying an argument's strengths, a writer may also notice the argument's weaknesses. Explain that a writer should not ignore these weaknesses. Instead, writers should include answers to possible objections in their essays. For example, *Some people may think kids should focus on academic subjects like math and reading, but technology can help teach these subjects, too.*

Guided Practice—We Do

Direct students to Activity 1 on handbook p. 61. Guide them to address possible weaknesses in the argument you planned together in Minilesson 47. For example, *Some people may think digital textbooks are expensive, but students can save money by renting them instead of paying full price to buy them.* Have students write in their books as you write on the board.

Practice/Apply—You Do

COLLABORATIVE Have pairs turn to Activity 2. Ask them to write statements that address possible weaknesses in their arguments.

INDEPENDENT Have students write statements that address possible weaknesses in the argument they planned for Activity 3.

Conference/Evaluate

As students draft, have them evaluate their work using the rubric on p. 104.

- eBook
- WriteSmart
- Interactive Lessons

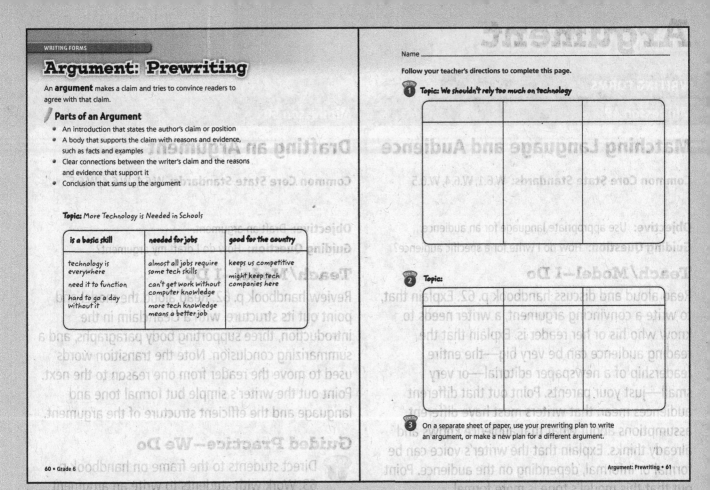

WRITING FORMS

Argument: Prewriting

An **argument** makes a claim and tries to convince readers to agree with that claim.

Parts of an Argument

- An introduction that states the author's claim or position
- A body that supports the claim with reasons and evidence, such as facts and examples
- Clear connections between the writer's claim and the reasons and evidence that support it
- Conclusion that sums up the argument

Topic: More Technology is Needed in Schools

is a basic skill	needed for jobs	good for the country
technology is everywhere need it to function hard to go a day without it	almost all jobs require some tech skills can't get work without computer knowledge more tech knowledge means a better job	keeps us competitive might keep tech companies here

60 • Grade 6

Name _____

Follow your teacher's directions to complete this page.

1 Topic: We shouldn't rely too much on technology

2 Topic:

3 On a separate sheet of paper, use your prewriting plan to write an argument, or make a new plan for a different argument.

Argument: Prewriting • 61

Corrective Feedback

IF . . . students are not able to address possible objections to their arguments,

THEN . . . have them discuss their topic with a partner. Encourage one student to write down objections to the other student's argument. Then have students write statements that respond to their partner's objections.

Focus Trait: Voice

When trying to persuade readers, a writer's voice should sound knowledgeable. Writers sound knowledgeable when they use examples that are relevant and specific.

To be relevant, evidence must be directly connected to the issue at hand. Suppose you are arguing that you should be allowed to get a cat. Which would be a better support: *cats are easy to take care of* or *cats are sometimes orange?* The first claim is more relevant, and therefore stronger.

Evidence should also be specific, because general claims are less convincing and can make the writer's voice seem uninformed. *Cats are easy to take care of* is not as convincing as *a cat only requires daily feeding and litter box maintenance*.

Suggest a broad topic, such as *Everyone should have a pet*. Have students suggest specific reasons and pieces of evidence to support it, such as *Taking a dog for a walk is a good way to get exercise*.

Grade 6 • **61**

Argument

Minilesson 49

Matching Language and Audience

Common Core State Standards: W.6.1, W.6.4, W.6.5

Objective: Use appropriate language for an audience.

Guiding Question: How do I write for a specific audience?

Teach/Model—I Do

Read aloud and discuss handbook p. 62. Explain that, to write a convincing argument, a writer needs to know who his or her reader is. Explain that the reading audience can be very big—the entire readership of a newspaper editorial—or very small—just your parents. Point out that different audiences mean that writers must have different assumptions about what that audience knows and already thinks. Explain that the writer's voice can be formal or informal, depending on the audience. Point out that this model's tone is more formal.

Guided Practice—We Do

Return to the argument about digital textbooks from Minilesson 47. Work together to write a list of possible audiences for that essay, ranging from classmates to parents to the community at large. Discuss how the same argument might be presented differently to each audience. Then guide students to determine what kind of language they would use for a particular audience, such as their classmates. Work together to make a list of words and phrases they might use in an essay.

Practice/Apply—You Do

COLLABORATIVE Have pairs choose a different potential audience from the list on the board. Have them make a list of words and phrases that fit with that audience.

INDEPENDENT Have students choose a different audience from the list and repeat the activity.

Conference/Evaluate

Circulate and help make sure students are using the appropriate level of formal or informal language.

Minilesson 50

Drafting an Argument

Common Core State Standards: W.6.1, W.6.4, W.6.5

Objective: Draft an argument.

Guiding Question: How do I draft my argument?

Teach/Model—I Do

Review handbook p. 62. Read aloud the model and point out its structure, with a clear claim in the introduction, three supporting body paragraphs, and a summarizing conclusion. Note the transition words used to move the reader from one reason to the next. Point out the writer's simple but formal tone and language and the efficient structure of the argument.

Guided Practice—We Do

 Direct students to the frame on handbook p. 63. Work with students to write an argument about an important technology skill. Work with students to come up with a topic and write an introductory sentence, such as *One important skill that every student must learn is how to type well.* Guide students to choose several reasons and facts. Work together to determine the audience for this piece, and encourage suggestions for how best to tailor the essay for that audience. Have students write in their books as you write on the board.

Practice/Apply—You Do

 COLLABORATIVE Have pairs plan and complete Activity 2. Tell them they can use their plans from the previous lesson or make a new plan.

 INDEPENDENT Have students read and follow the directions. Tell them to use their prewriting plan from the previous lesson or to create a new plan using Graphic Organizer 7.

Conference/Evaluate

As students draft, have them evaluate their work using the rubric on p. 104.

Digital
- eBook
- WriteSmart
- Interactive Lessons

Argument

An **argument** is an essay that tries to persuade readers to agree with the author's position.

Parts of an Argument

- Introduction that states the author's claim or position
- Body paragraphs that support the claim with reasons and evidence
- Conclusion that sums up the argument

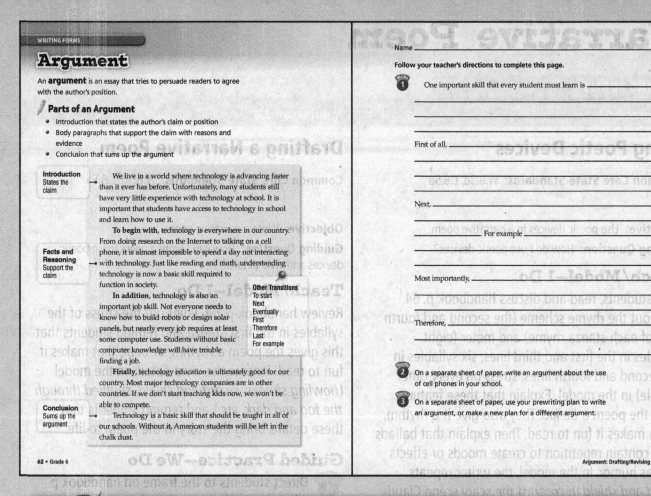

Introduction
States the claim

We live in a world where technology is advancing faster than it ever has before. Unfortunately, many students still have very little experience with technology at school. It is important that students have access to technology in school and learn how to use it.

Facts and Reasoning
Support the claim

To begin with, technology is everywhere in our country. From doing research on the Internet to talking on a cell phone, it is almost impossible to spend a day not interacting with technology. Just like reading and math, understanding technology is now a basic skill required to function in society.

In addition, technology is also an important job skill. Not everyone needs to know how to build robots or design solar panels, but nearly every job requires at least some computer use. Students without basic computer knowledge will have trouble finding a job.

Other Transitions
To start
Next
Eventually
First
Therefore
Last
For example

Finally, technology education is ultimately good for our country. Most major technology companies are in other countries. If we don't start teaching kids now, we won't be able to compete.

Conclusion
Sums up the argument

Technology is a basic skill that should be taught in all of our schools. Without it, American students will be left in the chalk dust.

62 • Grade 6

Name _____

Follow your teacher's directions to complete this page.

1 One important skill that every student must learn is _____

_____

First of all, _____

_____

Next, _____

_____

For example _____

_____

Most importantly, _____

_____

Therefore, _____

_____

2 On a separate sheet of paper, write an argument about the use of cell phones in your school.

3 On a separate sheet of paper, use your prewriting plan to write an argument, or make a new plan for a different argument.

Argument: Drafting/Revising • 63

Corrective Feedback

IF . . . students are using inappropriate language for their audience,

THEN . . . tell them to err on the side of formality when choosing a tone and style for an argument. When trying to persuade a reader, it is better to be too respectful and polished than not respectful and polished enough. Refer back to the list of possible audiences, and tell struggling students to write as if the audience was one notch more formal than the actual intended audience.

Focus Trait: Word Choice

Remind students that specific words can help a piece of writing sound more formal and persuasive or more chatty and informal. Write a few informal sentences on the board, such as:

Using a cell phone during class is totally lame. It's loud and obnoxious.

Listening to really loud music will blow out your eardrums. You gotta turn it down.

Ask students to think about whether these sentences are persuasive. Then work together to revise the sentences to be more formal. For example:

Using a cell phone during class is disruptive and bothers other students.

Consider turning down your music. If it is too loud, it could permanently damage your ears.

Have students compare the informal and the formal sentences. Ask students which they think is more persuasive and why.

Narrative Poem

Minilesson 51

Using Poetic Devices

Common Core State Standards: W.6.3d, L.6.5a

Objective: Use poetic devices in a narrative poem.
Guiding Question: How do I use poetic devices?

Teach/Model—I Do
With students, read and discuss handbook p. 64. Point out the rhyme scheme (the second and fourth lines of each stanza rhyme) and meter (eight syllables in the first and third lines; six syllables in the second and fourth lines; stress on every other syllable) in the model. Explain that these features make the poem a *ballad*. They also give it a rhythm, which makes it fun to read. Then explain that ballads often contain repetition to create moods or effects such as humor. In the model, the writer repeats s*word and shield* to contrast the scary scene Claude imagines with the reality of the raccoon. If possible, use a ballad such as "The Highwayman" to show an example of sentence repetition.

Guided Practice—We Do
Tell students you will write part of a narrative poem about exploring the desert. Together, write four lines, using the same rhyme and meter as the ballad on p. 64 (such as *Upon a barren desert dune,/the sand blew in my eyes./I whispered to my cousin Rex,/"This wasn't very wise!"*). Work with students to circle words you could repeat to create an eerie mood.

Practice/Apply—You Do
COLLABORATIVE Have pairs think of a different topic, such as *deep sea diving* or *meeting an unusual neighbor*. Have them write four lines with ballad rhyme and meter and circle words to repeat.

INDEPENDENT Have students choose a different topic and repeat the activity above.

Conference/Evaluate
If students are having trouble with meter, have them say the words aloud to a partner to hear the stresses.

Minilesson 52

Drafting a Narrative Poem

Common Core State Standards: W.6.3d, L.6.5a

Objective: Write a narrative poem.
Guiding Question: How can I write a poem using poetic devices and vivid details?

Teach/Model—I Do
Review handbook p. 64. Point out the stress of the syllables in the first stanza and remind students that this gives the poem a rhythm, or beat, that makes it fun to read. Review the vivid details in the model (*howling shrieks, sword and shield, shuffled through the fog and dark*, etc.) and remind students that these details bring the story in the poem to life.

Guided Practice—We Do
 Direct students to the frame on handbook p. 65. Call on volunteers to point out the meter in the poem by naming the stressed syllables (*fore, eyes, rene, held; ter, fy, sight*). Then, together, make a list of words that rhyme with *sight* and finish the first stanza with two lines that follow ballad meter and rhyme (Example: *A goblin blue it looked to be/That foraged in the night!*). Encourage students to develop the story in the poem by asking them questions, such as *Who is Irene? Is she alone? Is she outside or in her house?* Have students write in their books as you write on the board.

Practice/Apply—You Do
 COLLABORATIVE Have pairs plan and complete Activity 2. Encourage students to write a ballad, but allow them to write any narrative poem form they wish. Tell groups to share and discuss what they have written.

 INDEPENDENT Have students read and follow the directions for Activity 3.

Conference/Evaluate
As students draft, circulate and check meter. Evaluate using the rubric on p. 104.

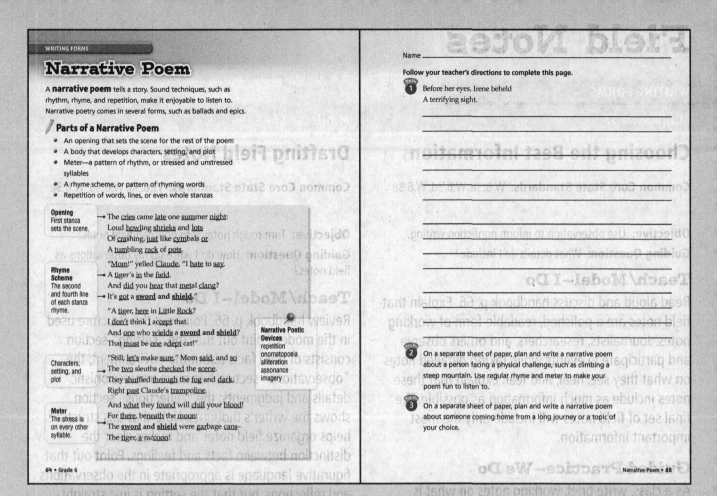

WRITING FORMS

Narrative Poem

A **narrative poem** tells a story. Sound techniques, such as rhythm, rhyme, and repetition, make it enjoyable to listen to. Narrative poetry comes in several forms, such as ballads and epics.

Parts of a Narrative Poem

- An opening that sets the scene for the rest of the poem
- A body that develops characters, setting, and plot
- Meter—a pattern of rhythm, or stressed and unstressed syllables
- A rhyme scheme, or pattern of rhyming words
- Repetition of words, lines, or even whole stanzas

Opening
First stanza sets the scene.

→ The <u>cries</u> came <u>late</u> one <u>summer</u> <u>night</u>:
Loud <u>howling shrieks</u> and <u>lots</u>
Of <u>crashing</u>, <u>just</u> like <u>cymbals</u> <u>or</u>
A <u>tumbling</u> <u>rack</u> of <u>pots</u>.

Rhyme Scheme
The second and fourth line of each stanza rhyme.

→ "<u>Mom</u>!" yelled <u>Claude</u>, "I <u>hate</u> to <u>say</u>,
A <u>tiger's</u> <u>in</u> the <u>field</u>.
And <u>did</u> you <u>hear</u> that <u>metal</u> <u>clang</u>?
→ It's <u>got</u> a <u>sword</u> and <u>shield</u>."

"A <u>tiger</u>, <u>here</u> in <u>Little</u> <u>Rock</u>?
I <u>don't</u> think <u>I</u> accept that.
And <u>one</u> who <u>wields</u> a **<u>sword</u>** and **<u>shield</u>**?
That <u>must</u> be <u>one</u> <u>adept</u> cat!"

Characters, setting, and plot

"Still, <u>let's</u> make <u>sure</u>," Mom <u>said</u>, and <u>so</u>
→ The <u>two</u> sleuths <u>checked</u> the <u>scene</u>.
They <u>shuffled</u> <u>through</u> the <u>fog</u> and <u>dark</u>,
Right <u>past</u> Claude's <u>trampoline</u>.

And <u>what</u> they <u>found</u> will <u>chill</u> your <u>blood</u>!
For <u>there</u>, beneath the <u>moon</u>:
The **<u>sword</u>** and **<u>shield</u>** were garbage <u>cans</u>—
The <u>tiger</u>, a <u>raccoon</u>!

Meter
The stress is on every other syllable.

Narrative Poetic Devices
repetition
onomatopoeia
alliteration
assonance
imagery

64 • Grade 6

Narrative Poem • 65

Name _____

Follow your teacher's directions to complete this page.

1 Before her eyes, Irene beheld
A terrifying sight.

_____
_____
_____
_____
_____
_____
_____
_____
_____
_____

2 On a separate sheet of paper, plan and write a narrative poem about a person facing a physical challenge, such as climbing a steep mountain. Use regular rhyme and meter to make your poem fun to listen to.

3 On a separate sheet of paper, plan and write a narrative poem about someone coming home from a long journey or a topic of your choice.

Corrective Feedback

IF . . . students have trouble writing a poem with a cohesive narrative,

THEN . . . have them use a story map to plan the poem as if it were a regular fictional narrative. Once they know what their plot, characters, and setting will be, they can turn it into a poem instead of a story.

Focus Trait: Word Choice

Remind students that figurative language, such as metaphors and similes, can make a poem more interesting. Explain that metaphors describe something but can't be literally true (example: *The snow was a thick down blanket covering the town*) and similes are comparisons (example: *Sarah's cough sounded like a seal barking*).

Give students a few bland sentences and ask them to add similes or metaphors. For example:

Irene yelled.

The goblin ran away.

Possible revisions:

Irene roared like a lion.

The monster was a race car speeding away.

Field Notes

Minilesson 53

Choosing the Best Information

Common Core State Standards: W.6.3a, W.6.3d, W.6.3e

Objective: Use observation to inform nonfiction writing.
Guiding Question: What details do I include?

Teach/Model—I Do

Read aloud and discuss handbook p. 66. Explain that field notes are a polished, readable form of working notes. Journalists, researchers, and others observe and participate in events while taking detailed notes on what they see, hear, and feel. Explain that these notes include as much information as possible. The final set of field notes will include only the most important information.

Guided Practice—We Do

As a class, write brief, working notes on what is happening at the moment. On the board, write down students' suggestions for describing the classroom, the people present, the situation, and the atmosphere. Remind students to use all of their senses. After the board is full, read through the notes with the class. Elicit recommendations for the most important notes, and circle them. Cross out observations that are redundant or unimportant. Have students save their notes.

Practice/Apply—You Do

COLLABORATIVE Have the class look out the window or take them outside. Have groups work together to take notes about what they see, including as much detail as possible. Then have them work together to circle important information and cross out anything unimportant or redundant.

INDEPENDENT Have students think about something they did in science class. Have them write notes, then choose what is important or unimportant.

Conference/Evaluate

Circulate and help students determine which observations are the most important.

Minilesson 54

Drafting Field Notes

Common Core State Standards: W.6.3a, W.6.3d, W.6.3e

Objective: Turn rough notes into polished field notes.
Guiding Question: How do I write up my observations as field notes?

Teach/Model—I Do

Review handbook p. 66. Point out the structure used in the model. Point out that the "setting" section consists of hard facts about the environment; the "observations" section has more impressionistic details and judgments; the "reflections" section shows the writer's thoughts. Note that this structure helps organize field notes and makes clear the distinction between facts and feelings. Point out that figurative language is appropriate in the observations and reflections, but that the setting is just straight-forward information.

Guided Practice—We Do

 Direct students to the frame on handbook p. 67. Work together to make notes about what is happening in the classroom or to use their notes from Minilesson 53 to draft more polished field notes. Guide students to include observations based on all five senses. Have students write in their books as you write on the board.

Practice/Apply—You Do

 COLLABORATIVE Have groups plan and complete Activity 2. They can use their notes from Minilesson 53 as a starting point. Have groups share their work.

 INDEPENDENT Have students read and follow the directions. Tell them to use their prewriting plan from Lesson 27 or to brainstorm a new plan using Graphic Organizer 15.

Conference/Evaluate

As students draft, have them evaluate their work using the rubric on p. 104.

Field Notes

Field notes are observations made "in the field" at a particular location—a park, a school, a library, or even a store or market.

Parts of Field Notes

- A record of sights, sounds, events, impressions, feelings, and questions
- An organization by category: Setting, Observations, Reflections
- Figurative language, such as similes, metaphors, and personification, to vividly express ideas

Setting
The *what, when, where, how long*

Observations
The events and the writer's impressions

Figurative Language
The words that vividly express the observations

Reflections
A summary of what the writer saw and heard

Setting: It is 9:30 on a Saturday morning and I'm watching my sister Petra's karate class. It's been thirty minutes, and the class is almost over. There are twelve students ranging in age from 7–12, one teacher, and an assistant. Most of the floor is covered with thick foam mats. Fifteen observers sit on a cold, hard, metal bench along one wall facing a row of mirrors on the other wall.

Observations: Petra is positioned in the middle of the front row. She is the youngest and smallest student, but she has the best concentration. Her eyes focus like a cat waiting to pounce, and her stance is strong as steel. Balancing on her right leg, she doesn't move. She is a statue—unwavering, unchanging. The student next to her splats on the floor like a bug on a windshield, but Petra doesn't flinch. The sensei calls out numbers, and Petra performs the moves flawlessly. Downward block, front punch, rising block, "Ki-Yi!" Reflected in the mirror is seemingly effortless coordination, steady and graceful as a dancer.

Other Figurative Phrases
leaves dance in the wind
quiet as a falling feather
he is a turbulent ocean

Reflections: Karate isn't really about fighting but concentration and discipline. To succeed, you have to be able to tune out everything going on around you and focus on your current task. I wonder if Petra will always have such dedication.

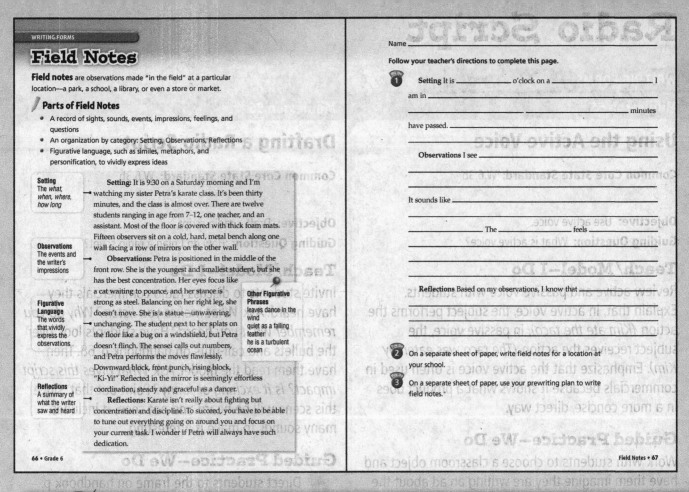

Follow your teacher's directions to complete this page.

1 **Setting** It is _____ o'clock on a _____ I am in _____

_____ _____ minutes have passed. _____

Observations I see _____

_____

It sounds like _____

_____ The _____ feels _____

_____

Reflections Based on my observations, I know that _____

2 On a separate sheet of paper, write field notes for a location at your school.

3 On a separate sheet of paper, use your prewriting plan to write field notes.

✓ Corrective Feedback

IF . . . students are having a hard time identifying important and vivid details,

THEN . . . have them make a chart that includes the five Ws (who, what, where, when, why) and the five senses. Tell students to include at least one fact or observation for each of the Ws and senses.

Focus Trait: Voice

Students may find it difficult to separate facts from subjective observations in their field notes. Explain that facts are provable. For example, *the party was in the gymnasium, the whole sixth grade was in attendance, refreshments were served.* Help students to see the distinction between these facts and subjective observations, like *the decorations were attractive, the music was great for dancing,* and *the refreshments were delicious.*

Explore different ways to make this distinction clear through the writer's tone. Ask students to make two columns to organize observations from their field work. One column should be for facts, the other for subjective observations. Demonstrate to students that it is appropriate to use figurative language and opinions in writing up the subjective observations, but that facts should speak for themselves.

Radio Script

Minilesson 55	Minilesson 56

Using the Active Voice

Common Core State Standard: W.6.3b

Objective: Use active voice.
Guiding Question: What is active voice?

Teach/Model—I Do

Review active and passive voice with students. Explain that, in active voice, the subject performs the action *(Kim ate the taco)*; in passive voice, the subject receives the action *(The taco was eaten by Kim)*. Emphasize that the active voice is often used in commercials because it shows what a product does in a more concise, direct way.

Guided Practice—We Do

Work with students to choose a classroom object and have them imagine they are writing an ad about the object. Write a few sentences about it using the active voice. For example, *The eraser glides over the board. It wipes away all the text.* Guide students to avoid passive-voice sentences, such as *The text is erased.* Remind students that using active voice is more direct and easier to understand.

Practice/Apply—You Do

COLLABORATIVE Ask students to work in groups to develop three sentences for an imaginary ad about an everyday household object. Remind them to use active voice.

INDEPENDENT Have students choose another object to write an ad about. Have them work independently to write three sentences using the active voice.

Conference/Evaluate

Remind students that they can identify active and passive voice by asking themselves this question: *Who is doing what to whom?*

Drafting a Radio Script

Common Core State Standard: W.6.3b

Objective: Draft a radio script.
Guiding Question: How do I plan a radio script?

Teach/Model—I Do

Invite students to discuss radio commercials they have heard. Ask *What makes you listen? Why do you remember what you heard?* Have students look over the bullets and call-outs on handbook p. 68. Then have them read the model. Ask *What gives this script impact? Is it exciting or funny?* Point out that, since this scene will be heard and not seen, it includes many sounds to make it interesting.

Guided Practice—We Do

 Direct students to the frame on handbook p. 69. Tell them that you will write a radio script together. Guide students to start by brainstorming a setting with distinctive sounds, such as a band practice room or zoo. Work together to start with a sound effect, such as *trombones bleating.* Together, write an opening sentence for the announcer, such as *Here we are at band practice for the Palmetto Middle School Band.* Have students write in their books as you write on the board.

Practice/Apply—You Do

 COLLABORATIVE Have groups plan and complete Activity 2. Remind them to emphasize the benefits of the product and to use the active voice.

 INDEPENDENT Have students read and follow the directions. Tell them to use their prewriting plan from Lesson 28 or to brainstorm a new plan using Graphic Organizer 7.

Conference/Evaluate

As students draft, have them evaluate their work using the rubric on p. 104.

Radio Script

A **radio script** seeks to convince listeners to buy a product.

Parts of a Radio Script

* A clear goal
* Reasons to buy the product
* A memorable take-away, or lasting impression
* May have an announcer, sound effects, voice-over, and characters
* Formal or informal voice as appropriate for subject and audience

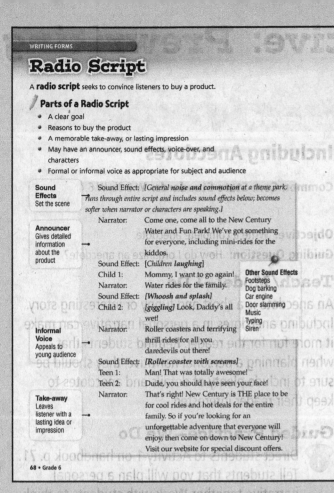

Sound Effects Set the scene	Sound Effect: [*General noise and commotion at a theme park, runs through entire script and includes sound effects below; becomes softer when narrator or characters are speaking.*]	
Announcer Gives detailed information about the product	Narrator: Come one, come all to the New Century Water and Fun Park! We've got something for everyone, including mini-rides for the kiddos.	
	Sound Effect: [*Children laughing*]	**Other Sound Effects**
	Child 1: Mommy, I want to go again!	Footsteps
	Narrator: Water rides for the family.	Dog barking
	Sound Effect: [*Whoosh and splash*]	Car engine
	Child 2: [*giggling*] Look, Daddy's all wet!	Door slamming
Informal Voice Appeals to young audience	Narrator: Roller coasters and terrifying thrill rides for all you daredevils out there!	Music Typing Siren
	Sound Effect: [*Roller coaster with screams*]	
	Teen 1: Man! That was totally awesome!	
	Teen 2: Dude, you should have seen your face!	
Take-away Leaves listener with a lasting idea or impression	Narrator: That's right! New Century is THE place to be for cool rides and hot deals for the entire family. So if you're looking for an unforgettable adventure that everyone will enjoy, then come on down to New Century! Visit our website for special discount offers.	

Name _____

Follow your teacher's directions to complete this page.

1 Sound Effect: _____

Announcer: _____
_____

Sound Effect: _____
_____
_____

Announcer: _____
_____

Sound Effect: _____
_____

Announcer: _____
_____

2 On a separate sheet of paper, write a radio script for a product that you use.

3 On a separate sheet of paper, use your prewriting plan to write a radio script, or make a new plan for a different product.

Corrective Feedback

IF . . . students have difficulty distinguishing active from passive voice,

THEN . . . tell them to ask *Who is doing what to whom?* In the active voice, the subject of the sentence is doing the action. In the passive voice, the doer often comes after the verb, usually in a prepositional phrase. For example, *The narrator read the script* is active. *The script was read by the narrator* is passive. Explain that sometimes in passive voice, the doer is never mentioned. For example: *The script was read* and *The chair was broken.*

Focus Trait: Sentence Fluency

Direct students' attention to the dialogue in the model script on handbook p. 68. Ask *Does this dialogue sound natural?*

Remind students that dialogue imitates the way people actually talk. It uses the words and rhythms of everyday speech.

One good way to test dialogue is to read it aloud. If the words flow easily off a reader's tongue, the dialogue probably sounds natural. If a reader stumbles, the sentences may need to be revised.

Another way to test dialogue is to ask if it matches the way readers would expect a character to speak. For example, does the line spoken by Child 1 in the model script actually sound like a child?

Have students practice writing natural dialogue by suggesting what parents and senior citizens might say in a longer commercial about the fun park.

Personal Narrative: Prewriting

Minilesson 57

Planning a Sequence of Events

Common Core State Standards: W.6.3a, W.6.4

Objective: Develop a well-structured narrative.

Guiding Question: How can I put events in logical order?

Teach/Model—I Do

On the board, write the sentences from the graphic organizer on p. 70 out of order. Ask *What makes this story confusing?* Point out that the events are confusing because they are out of sequence. Then point to p. 70 and have students read the organizer. Guide students to add words like *first* and *second* to show the sequence of events.

Guided Practice—We Do

Write an introductory sentence on the board, such as, *"How hard can it be to fix a hot breakfast?" asked my father.* Leave space for 3–4 events. Then write a conclusion: *After the smoke cleared, we decided that cold cereal would make a great breakfast after all.* Work with students to add 3–4 events in a logical order.

Practice/Apply—You Do

COLLABORATIVE Have groups choose another topic for a narrative. Have groups work together to come up with 3–5 events for a narrative and to write those events in a logical order.

INDEPENDENT Have students choose another topic for a narrative. Have them think of 3–5 events and write them in a logical order.

Conference/Evaluate

Circulate and help students put their events in order by asking questions, such as *Does it make sense for this event to happen first? What happens next?*

Minilesson 58

Including Anecdotes

Common Core State Standards: W.6.3b, W.6.4

Objective: Write a complete anecdote.

Guiding Question: How do I organize an anecdote?

Teach/Model—I Do

An anecdote is a short and funny or interesting story. Including anecdotes in a personal narrative can make it more fun for the reader. Remind students that, when planning a personal narrative, they should be sure to include plenty of details and anecdotes to keep their reader interested.

Guided Practice—We Do

 Direct students to Activity 1 on handbook p. 71. Tell students that you will plan a personal narrative together. Work with students to think of a time they tried something new. Guide students to choose one topic and work together to think of events to fill in the flow chart, such as *The first time I went to an amusement park, I was afraid to get on a roller coaster.* Have students write in their books as you write on the board.

Practice/Apply—You Do

 COLLABORATIVE Have groups plan and complete Activity 2. Tell them to use words like *first, next,* and *afterward* to show the order in which events happened.

 INDEPENDENT Have students read and follow the directions. Tell them to use their prewriting plan from Lesson 29 or to brainstorm a new plan using a flow chart like the one on p. 71.

Conference/Evaluate

As students draft, have them evaluate their work using the rubric on p. 104.

- eBook
- WriteSmart
- Interactive Lessons

Personal Narrative: Prewriting

A **personal narrative** is a true story about the writer's life.

Parts of a Personal Narrative

- A beginning that catches the reader's attention
- A middle that explains the events in sequential (time) order
- An ending that wraps up events and tells how the writer felt
- Events told in the first-person point of view
- Vivid words that show the writer's personality

> I was excited and nervous to try kayaking for the first time.

> I got in the boat without tipping, but it was still wobbly.

> I tried my first roll and made it all the way around.

> I tried a second roll, got stuck under water, and had to swim out.

> We practiced rolling until everyone could do it.

> Then we took a trip down the creek.

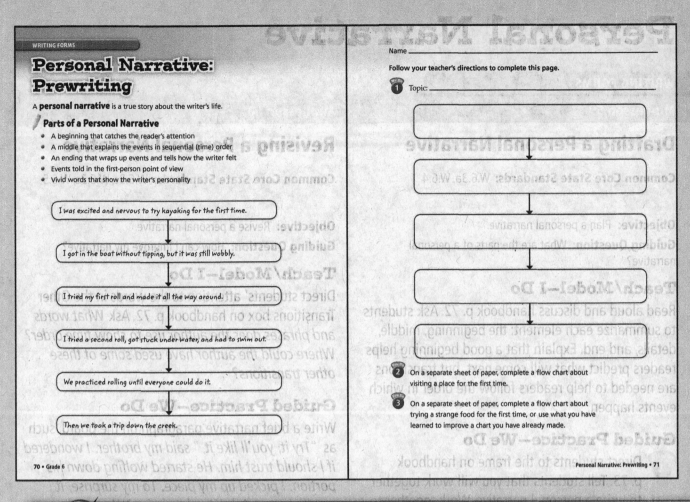

Name _____

Follow your teacher's directions to complete this page.

1 Topic: _____

 2 On a separate sheet of paper, complete a flow chart about visiting a place for the first time.

3 On a separate sheet of paper, complete a flow chart about trying a strange food for the first time, or use what you have learned to improve a chart you have already made.

✓ Corrective Feedback

IF . . . students have trouble thinking of anecdotes to include in their personal narratives,

THEN . . . remind them that an anecdote should focus on the most interesting event of the experience. Have them imagine sharing their story with a friend. Ask *What part of this experience would entertain your friend the most? What part would make your friend laugh or keep them interested?*

Focus Trait: Sentence Fluency

Remind students that using transitions like *first, afterwards,* and *immediately* helps readers follow the sequence of events in an anecdote or narrative.

Discuss what happens if writers start every sentence in a narrative with *first, second, third,* and similar transitions. The order of events is clear, but readers may be bored because every sentence begins the same way. Explain that transitions can be used not just in the beginning of a sentence, but also in the middle or end.

Direct students' attention to handbook p. 70. Ask *Where do you find the words that show time order?* Point out that instead of writing, *First, I tried a roll...,* the author writes *I tried my first roll.*
Challenge students to rewrite these sentences:

First, you must catch the dog to give him a bath.

Next, you have the challenge of getting him wet.

After that, soap suds fly everywhere.

Finally, you need a towel to dry yourself off.

Grade 6 • 71

Personal Narrative

Minilesson 59

Drafting a Personal Narrative

Common Core State Standards: W.6.3a, W.6.4

Objective: Plan a personal narrative.

Guiding Question: What are the parts of a personal narrative?

Teach/Model—I Do

Read aloud and discuss handbook p. 72. Ask students to summarize each element: the beginning, middle, details, and end. Explain that a good beginning helps readers predict what will come next, but transitions are needed to help readers follow the order in which events happen.

Guided Practice—We Do

Direct students to the frame on handbook p. 73. Tell students that you will work together to write a personal narrative. Work together to use their plan from Minilesson 58 or to come up with a new plan for a narrative about a time they tried something new. Start by writing an opening sentence, such as *I was really excited about riding a roller coaster.* Then complete the frame together. Have students write in their books as you write on the board.

Practice/Apply—You Do

COLLABORATIVE Have groups plan and complete Activity 2. Remind them to write events in a logical sequence.

INDEPENDENT Have students read and follow the directions. Tell them to use their prewriting plan from the previous lesson or to create a new plan in a flow chart.

Conference/Evaluate

As students draft, have them evaluate their work using the rubric on p. 104.

Minilesson 60

Revising a Personal Narrative

Common Core State Standards: W.6.3c, W.6.3e, W.6.5

Objective: Revise a personal narrative.

Guiding Question: How can I improve my narrative?

Teach/Model—I Do

Direct students' attention to the words in the Other Transitions box on handbook p. 72. Ask *What words and phrases does the author use to show time order? Where could the author have used some of these other transitions?*

Guided Practice—We Do

Write a brief narrative paragraph on the board, such as *"Try it; you'll like it," said my brother. I wondered if I should trust him. He started wolfing down his portion. I picked up my piece. To my surprise, it smelled good.* Ask *What's missing?* Work with students to revise this draft to add details about what the narrator is eating. Then guide them to add transitions between the sentences to help the narrative flow more smoothly. Remind them to use editor's marks as they revise.

Practice/Apply—You Do

COLLABORATIVE Ask students to work in groups to revise their drafts from Minilesson 59. Remind them to use transition words, add details, and make sure their events are told in a logical order.

INDEPENDENT Have students revise a different draft of a personal narrative. Remind them to move sentences that are out of order and to add transition words. Remind them to use editor's marks.

Conference/Evaluate

Have students review their revised drafts to be sure events are told in a logical order.

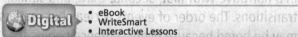
Digital • eBook • WriteSmart • Interactive Lessons

Personal Narrative

A **personal narrative** tells about a real experience from the writer's life.

Parts of a Personal Narrative

- A beginning that draws readers in
- A middle that describes the experience in time order, or sequence
- An ending that tells how the events worked out or how the writer felt
- Events told in the first-person point of view
- Precise words and descriptive details that show the writer's personality

Beginning Description that draws readers in	I had never been in a kayak before, so I was really excited to try it. I was scared, too. I knew kayaks could roll over, but I didn't know how to get out when they did.
Middle Describes events in time order	**First** we had to get into the boat without tipping it over. My kayak had a pretty flat bottom, but it still felt really wobbly. Even though the water was cold, I was sweating! **When** we were all seated in the little boats, the instructor told us we would learn to roll. We'd turn the kayaks over on purpose! Then we'd roll them upright again. If we couldn't roll, we would slip out of the seat and swim the kayak to shore. I took a deep, shaky breath and rolled.
Details that show what the writer is like	There I was, upside down in my kayak! My lungs felt like they would burst. I'd rolled hard enough, though. My kayak popped upright. I felt really proud to have done it right -- until my second try! That time I got stuck upside down underwater. I got water up my nose, and I had to swim out.
Ending Wraps up the narrative and tells how the writer felt	We rolled the kayaks over and over. **Finally,** everyone could do it, and we were ready to head down the creek. I couldn't believe I learned how to roll a kayak in just one day!

Other Transitions
When it started
After that
Next
Also
Soon
Before long
In the end

Name _____

Follow your teacher's directions to complete this page.

 I was really excited about _____
_____ First, _____
_____
_____ When _____
_____
_____
Later on, _____
_____
_____
What surprised me was _____
_____
_____
_____
_____
Finally, _____
_____
_____

2 On a separate sheet of paper, write a personal narrative about visiting a place for the first time.

3 On a separate sheet of paper, use your prewriting plan to write a personal narrative, or plan and write a personal narrative about trying a strange food for the first time.

✓ Corrective Feedback

IF . . . students find it difficult to sequence events in a logical order,

THEN . . . ask them to use note cards or sticky notes to write down everything that might happen. Have them rearrange their notes until they find a logical order.

Focus Trait: Organization

Tell students that the beginning sentence of a narrative sets up an expectation. Direct their attention to the first sentence in the model on handbook p. 72. Discuss some of the expectations the sentence creates. For example, readers can predict that the narrative will be about learning to kayak, that the setting will be near water, and that the narrator will have to learn how to roll over.

List the expectations students mention on the board. Ask *How does the middle of the narrative meet*

these expectations? Have students identify details that address each expectation they listed.

Ask *How are the beginning and ending related?* Guide students to see that at the beginning the writer is looking forward to learning to kayak. At the end, the writer sums up what was learned. Personal narratives often end by summing up what the writer learned, how the writer changed, or how the writer feels about what happened.

Prewriting

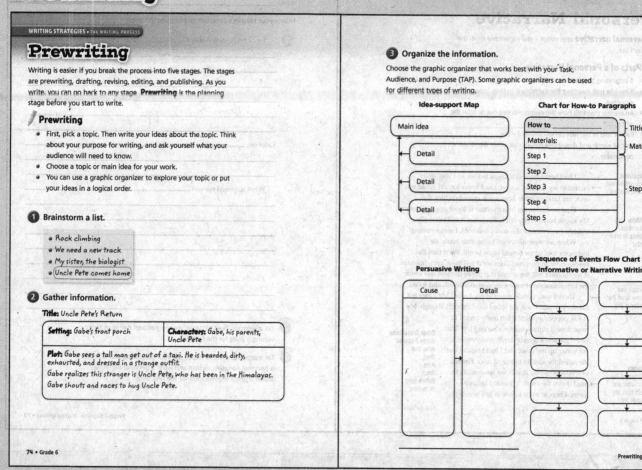

Prewriting

Writing is easier if you break the process into five stages. The stages are prewriting, drafting, revising, editing, and publishing. As you write, you can go back to any stage. **Prewriting** is the planning stage before you start to write.

Prewriting

- First, pick a topic. Then write your ideas about the topic. Think about your purpose for writing, and ask yourself what your audience will need to know.
- Choose a topic or main idea for your work.
- You can use a graphic organizer to explore your topic or put your ideas in a logical order.

1 Brainstorm a list.

- Rock climbing
- We need a new track
- My sister, the biologist
- Uncle Pete comes home

2 Gather information.

Title: Uncle Pete's Return

Setting: Gabe's front porch	**Characters:** Gabe, his parents, Uncle Pete

Plot: Gabe sees a tall man get out of a taxi. He is bearded, dirty, exhausted, and dressed in a strange outfit.
Gabe realizes this stranger is Uncle Pete, who has been in the Himalayas. Gabe shouts and races to hug Uncle Pete.

3 Organize the information.

Choose the graphic organizer that works best with your Task, Audience, and Purpose (TAP). Some graphic organizers can be used for different types of writing.

Idea-support Map

Main idea → Detail → Detail → Detail

Chart for How-to Paragraphs

How to _____ – Title
Materials: – Materials
Step 1
Step 2
Step 3 – Steps
Step 4
Step 5

Persuasive Writing

Cause | Detail

Sequence of Events Flow Chart for Informative or Narrative Writing

74 • Grade 6

Prewriting • 75

WRITING STRATEGY

Minilesson 61

Introducing Prewriting

Common Core State Standards: W.6.4, W.6.5

Objective: Understand why and how to prewrite.

Guiding Question: How can I use these pages to help me plan a good essay?

Teach/Model

Have students read the explanation of prewriting on p. 74. Explain the stages of the writing process, emphasizing that prewriting is the starting point for the other steps. Point out that prewriting will make the drafting stage easier and faster.

Practice/Apply

Give students a sample topic and have them brainstorm a list of ideas for an essay. Tell students to compare and discuss their brainstorm lists.

Minilesson 62

Choosing The Right Organizer

Common Core State Standards: W.6.4, W.6.5

Objective: Use graphic organizers for prewriting.

Guiding Question: How do I pick which graphic organizer to use for my essay?

Teach/Model

Explain to students that different graphic organizers are better for each kind of writing. Discuss the different tasks, audiences, and purposes (TAPs) a writer might have for a project, and point out that prewriting should focus on these elements.

Practice/Apply

Have students discuss the graphic organizers on p. 75 and list one possible writing topic that would be well-served by each organizer.

Drafting

Drafting

Drafting is the second step of the writing process. When you draft, you use your prewriting plan to write what you planned.

Drafting

- Sometimes your plan or graphic organizer has all the information you need. Write your main ideas and details as complete sentences.
- At other times, you may need to expand your ideas further. For example, add vivid description and details to a narrative.
- Organize your writing logically. For example, group related ideas in a paragraph with a topic sentence.

Narrative

Title: Uncle Pete's Return

Setting: Gabe's front porch	**Characters:** Gabe, his parents, Uncle Pete

Plot: Gabe sees a tall man get out of a taxi. He is bearded, dirty, exhausted, and dressed in a strange outfit.

Gabe realizes this stranger is Uncle Pete, who has been in the Himalayas.

Gabe shouts and races to hug Uncle Pete.

Draft

The stranger was tall, bearded, and as dirty as a toddler who had been playing in the mud. His face above the scraggly beard looked exhausted. There were dark circles under his green eyes. He looked like he hadn't eaten a good meal in weeks. He was wearing a shirt with many colors and unusual patterns on it.

Persuasive

Topic: We need a new track.

Opinion: School's track should be replaced.

Reason: Track team deserves better facilities.

Reason: Other people could use track.

Reason: We spend lots of money on other programs.

Draft

Our school needs to replace our crumbly, worn-out track right away. For one thing, our track team deserves a better place to practice. The team is very talented, but we have a hard time running on the old track. How will we have a chance at another league championship if we're always slipping on the starting line?

WRITING STRATEGY

Minilesson 63

Understanding Drafting

Common Core State Standard: W.6.5

Objective: Understand the purpose of the drafting step.

Guiding Question: Why should I draft?

Teach/Model

Have students read the definition and bulleted points. Explain that drafting is the second stage of the writing process, when writers begin to write complete sentences and paragraphs. Emphasize that a draft does not have to be perfect. Tell students they can fix their mistakes later.

Practice/Apply

Discuss with students how the model writer took the ideas from the organizer shown on p. 76 and drafted a story.

Minilesson 64

Going from Organizer to Draft

Common Core State Standard: W.6.5

Objective: Transition from the organizer to the draft.

Guiding Question: How do I turn my prewriting into a draft?

Teach/Model

Read the model drafts with students. Point out how the writer used the ideas shown in the graphic organizers to write sentences and paragraphs. Then show students that the writers also added details and developed ideas when they wrote their drafts.

Practice/Apply

Have students choose an outline or graphic organizer from a piece of writing they have already planned and discuss how they can take the ideas in the organizer to draft a paragraph.

Revising

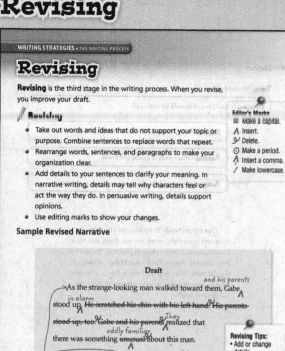

WRITING STRATEGIES • THE WRITING PROCESS

Revising

Revising is the third stage in the writing process. When you revise, you improve your draft.

Revising

- Take out words and ideas that do not support your topic or purpose. Combine sentences to replace words that repeat.
- Rearrange words, sentences, and paragraphs to make your organization clear.
- Add details to your sentences to clarify your meaning. In narrative writing, details may tell why characters feel or act the way they do. In persuasive writing, details support opinions.
- Use editing marks to show your changes.

Editor's Marks
≡ Make a capital.
∧ Insert.
⌘ Delete.
⊙ Make a period.
⋏ Insert a comma.
/ Make lowercase.

Sample Revised Narrative

Draft

As the strange-looking man walked toward them, Gabe and his parents
stood up. He scratched his chin with his left hand. His parents
stood up, too. Gabe and his parents realized that
there was something unusual about this man.

Gabe was afraid at first. Gabe thought he recognized
him.

Revising Tips:
- Add or change details.
- Move sentences for clarity.
- Combine sentences.
- Delete unnecessary details.

78 • Grade 6

Other Ways to Revise

- Add transition words to make sentences and ideas flow more smoothly.
- Replace dull or vague words with more vivid and specific words.
- Add dialogue or quotations to make your narrative or essay more interesting.
- Rewrite unexciting sentences to show your voice and personality.

Sample Revised Persuasive Essay

Draft

students at our school and members of our community
Other people could use the track, too. The soccer team
Then they wouldn't
could do their warm-ups on the track. They do passing and
have to run laps around the parking lot. and football
shooting drills on the soccer field. The baseball team can use
the track to practice running. The football team can use the
Runners
track to practice. Other people from the community can use the
track to run when the sports teams aren't using it.

Revising • 79

WRITING STRATEGY

Minilesson 65

Understanding Revising

Common Core State Standard: W.6.5

Objective: Understand the purpose and techniques of revision.

Guiding Question: How do I improve my first draft?

Teach/Model

Review p. 78 with students. Explain that during revision, a writer makes careful changes to improve a draft. Explain that the use of editor's marks allows a writer to see the development of their work. Note that when using a word processor, the track changes function can be used similarly.

Practice/Apply

Have students revise a short piece of their own writing using standard editor's marks. Have them compare revisions with a neighbor.

Minilesson 66

Revising Different Kinds of Writing

Common Core State Standard: W.6.5

Objective: Revise different kinds of writing.

Guiding Question: How do I revise my writing?

Teach/Model

Read p. 79 with students. Explain that persuasive writing should have specific examples and clarify arguments, while revising a narrative might focus on adding detail and clarifying the story. Discuss the different kinds of writing.

Practice/Apply

Have students select a piece of their own writing and discuss how they can revise it to improve organization and clarity.

Editing and Publishing

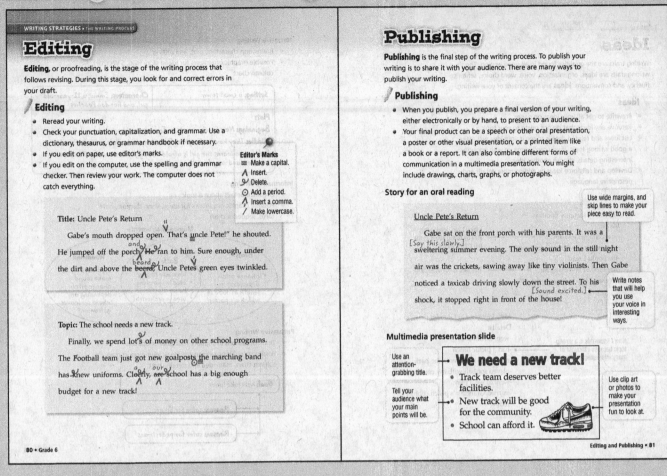

Minilesson 67

Understanding Editing

Common Core State Standard: W.6.5

Objective: Understand how to proofread a revised draft.

Guiding Question: What is the difference between revising and editing?

Teach/Model

Have students read p. 80. Explain that editing focuses on spelling, grammar, punctuation, and other conventions, whereas revising is about changing ideas. Remind students that a computer spellcheck is not enough to find all of their mistakes.

Practice/Apply

Point out the errors marked in the model on p. 80. Discuss why each mistake is incorrect and how the writer made changes to improve the draft.

Minilesson 68

Understanding Publishing

Common Core State Standard: W.6.5

Objective: Understand how to publish writing.

Guiding Question: What do I do with my writing when it is complete?

Teach/Model

Explain to students that the final step of writing is to share the work with the audience. Offer examples of audiences and ways of sharing work. Note that even a simple publication, like printing out an essay for a teacher, requires clean formatting for easy reading.

Practice/Apply

Have students discuss ways to publish their work, such as making posters, giving presentations, or displaying it for the class.

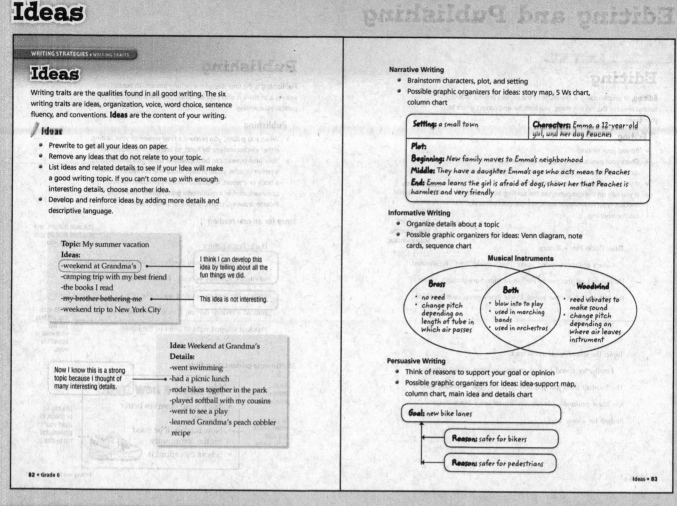

Minilesson 69

Understanding Ideas

Common Core State Standards: W.6.4, W.6.5

Objective: Understand how to brainstorm ideas.

Guiding Question: How can I find good ideas for my writing?

Teach/Model

Have students read the definition and bulleted points on p. 82. Add that part of prewriting is brainstorming ideas for writing. Explain that students should write down everything that comes to mind. Later, they will decide which ideas to use.

Practice/Apply

Assign students general topics like *beach trip* or *bake sales* and ask them to brainstorm ideas for any form of writing on that topic.

Minilesson 70

Using a Graphic Organizer

Common Core State Standards: W.6.4, W.6.5

Objective: Use graphic organizers to prewrite ideas.

Guiding Question: How do I evaluate my ideas?

Teach/Model

With students, study the organizers on pp. 82–83. Explain that the organizers can help them evaluate their ideas. For example, if they begin a Venn diagram and can only generate similarities, they either need to do further research or choose a different topic.

Practice/Apply

Have students brainstorm ideas on a general topic, such as *favorite foods* or *U.S. states,* and then evaluate them using one of the graphic organizers on p. 83.

Organization

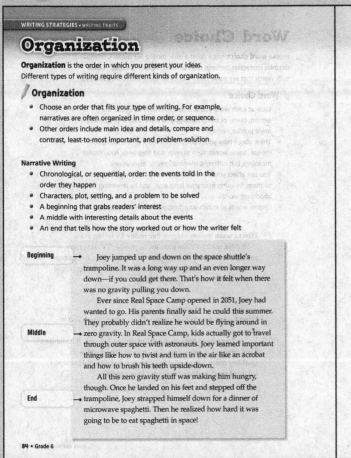

WRITING STRATEGIES • WRITING TRAITS

Organization

Organization is the order in which you present your ideas. Different types of writing require different kinds of organization.

Organization

- Choose an order that fits your type of writing. For example, narratives are often organized in time order, or sequence.
- Other orders include main idea and details, compare and contrast, least-to-most important, and problem-solution.

Narrative Writing
- Chronological, or sequential, order: the events told in the order they happen
- Characters, plot, setting, and a problem to be solved
- A beginning that grabs readers' interest
- A middle with interesting details about the events
- An end that tells how the story worked out or how the writer felt

Beginning → Joey jumped up and down on the space shuttle's trampoline. It was a long way up and an even longer way down—if you could get there. That's how it felt when there was no gravity pulling you down.

Middle → Ever since Real Space Camp opened in 2051, Joey had wanted to go. His parents finally said he could this summer. They probably didn't realize he would be flying around in zero gravity. In Real Space Camp, kids actually got to travel through outer space with astronauts. Joey learned important things like how to twist and turn in the air like an acrobat and how to brush his teeth upside-down.

End → All this zero gravity stuff was making him hungry, though. Once he landed on his feet and stepped off the trampoline, Joey strapped himself down for a dinner of microwave spaghetti. Then he realized how hard it was going to be to eat spaghetti in space!

84 • Grade 6

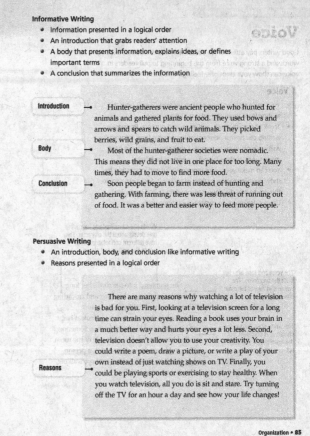

Informative Writing
- Information presented in a logical order
- An introduction that grabs readers' attention
- A body that presents information, explains ideas, or defines important terms
- A conclusion that summarizes the information

Introduction → Hunter-gatherers were ancient people who hunted for animals and gathered plants for food. They used bows and arrows and spears to catch wild animals. They picked berries, wild grains, and fruit to eat.

Body → Most of the hunter-gatherer societies were nomadic. This means they did not live in one place for too long. Many times, they had to move to find more food.

Conclusion → Soon people began to farm instead of hunting and gathering. With farming, there was less threat of running out of food. It was a better and easier way to feed more people.

Persuasive Writing
- An introduction, body, and conclusion like informative writing
- Reasons presented in a logical order

Reasons → There are many reasons why watching a lot of television is bad for you. First, looking at a television screen for a long time can strain your eyes. Reading a book uses your brain in a much better way and hurts your eyes a lot less. Second, television doesn't allow you to use your creativity. You could write a poem, draw a picture, or write a play of your own instead of just watching shows on TV. Finally, you could be playing sports or exercising to stay healthy. When you watch television, all you do is sit and stare. Try turning off the TV for an hour a day and see how your life changes!

Organization • 85

Minilesson 71

Understanding Organization

Common Core State Standards: W.6.1a, W.6.4, W.6.5

Objective: Understand how to organize writing.

Guiding Question: How do I decide what part comes next?

Teach/Model

With students, read the definition and bulleted list on pp. 84–85. Explain that organizing details in a logical order will help their readers understand their writing better. Writers choose the best organization to suit their purpose for writing, such as placing events in the order they happened in a narrative.

Practice/Apply

Ask students to work together to brainstorm different ways the story of Cinderella could be organized. Discuss how reordering events would change how the story affects the reader.

Minilesson 72

Organizing Ideas

Common Core State Standards: W.6.4, W.6.5

Objective: Understand organization for different kinds of writing.

Guiding Question: How do I organize my writing?

Teach/Model

Have students read the models and bullets. Point out the different organizational structures in each model. Call students' attention to the order of events in the narrative, the order of details in the informational paragraph, and the order of reasons in the persuasive paragraph.

Practice/Apply

Have students look at the persuasive model on p. 85. Discuss how else this paragraph could be organized.

Writing for Common Core • 79

Voice and Word Choice

WRITING STRATEGIES • WRITING TRAITS

Voice

Good writers pay attention to **voice**. They use descriptive, exciting words and a strong voice from the beginning to pull readers in. Your voice can show your emotions, feelings, and personality.

Voice

- Your voice sets the tone of your writing. Tone is how the author feels about the subject and audience.
- Think about your task, audience, and purpose. Persuasive writing can have a personal or impersonal tone. Informative writing is often more formal. Expressive writing can have many tones, such as friendly, warm, or humorous.
- You can make your voice more colorful and interesting by showing information instead of telling it. Some ways to do this are to add dialogue, sensory details, and examples.
- Use precise words to create your unique voice.

The voice and tone are clear from the beginning. The writer is in awe of the main character.

The writer does not say the character is confident, but the word choice and voice tell us what she is like.

Words like *sauntered* and *cascading* give details about the character. They have different connotations from words like *walked* and *falling*.

She sauntered into the room, her long brown hair flowing behind her and cascading down onto her brightly colored shirt. Everyone in the room turned to look at her. She just had that kind of presence. Someone called her name on the other side of the room. She could have looked toward that person, but she didn't need to. She just kept walking, slowly and purposefully.

86 • Grade 6

Word Choice

Precise **word choice** helps paint a clear picture for readers. It helps describe characters, settings, and actions. Replacing unclear words with words that are more exact makes for more interesting reading.

Word Choice

- Look at each word you use. See if it really describes the person, place, or thing the way you want it to. If you can be more precise, revise.
- Think about how your audience will react to the words you choose. Some words, such as *odor* and *fragrance*, have similar meanings but different connotations, or associations.
- You can affect your readers' reaction by speaking directly to them, by using figurative language, and by repeating important words.
- Choose words to match your task, audience, and purpose.

Effect I want: readers to agree that reality TV is disgusting

I think reality TV has gone too far. Reality TV shows are garbage for the eyes. Garbage goes into these shows, and garbage comes out. Do we really need to waste our time watching people behave badly?

Effect I want: readers to understand how incredible my visit to Bruges was

As I wandered through the city of Bruges, Belgium, the Middle Ages came to life around me. The city was like a jewel, with sparkling canals, step-roofed brick houses, and peaceful gardens. I felt that I was wandering through a long-ago time.

Voice and Word Choice • 87

WRITING STRATEGY

Minilesson 73

Understanding Voice

Common Core State Standard: W.6.4

Objective: Develop a unique voice as a writer.

Guiding Question: How can I give my writing more personality?

Teach/Model

Have students read p. 86. Add that voice is the distinctive quality that each writer brings to her work. Explain that voice can sound different for different purposes and audiences.

Practice/Apply

Have students read excerpts from familiar books or sample essays and describe the writer's voice in each excerpt.

Minilesson 74

Understanding Word Choice

Common Core State Standard: W.6.4

Objective: Use specific and evocative words.

Guiding Question: How do I find the words that best suit my meaning?

Teach/Model

Explain that words have shades of meaning and writers should choose their words carefully to help make their meaning clear. Suggest that students use a thesaurus to help find exact words.

Practice/Apply

On the board, write a sentence with vague or dull words, such as *We went to the place and ate some food.* Work together to rewrite the sentence using more exact words, such as *We went to the fair and ate some popcorn.*

Sentence Fluency

WRITING STRATEGIES • WRITING TRAITS

Sentence Fluency

Sentence fluency makes your writing more readable. Correct, flowing sentences make your writing clearer and more interesting for readers.

Sentence Fluency

- Combine short, choppy sentences for smoother writing.
- Use different kinds of sentences; not all sentences need to be declarative. Also, vary your sentence structures. Include simple, compound, complex, and compound-complex sentences.

Same Kind of Sentences
It was time for Anna to go home. She was tired. She had been working on the project all day. She had hardly made a dent in the work. She was the only one who could do the project on time. Anna was glad it was her last assignment.

Sentence Variety
Anna was tired and knew it was time to go home. Even though she had been working on the project all day, she had hardly made a dent in it. Was she really the only one who could get it done on time? She said quietly to herself, "I'm so glad this is my last assignment!"

Choppy Sentences
Frank stared at the dirty walls. He stirred the paint. He had to wash the walls. He filled a bucket with water and special soap. He scrubbed hard. The walls were clean. He started to paint.

Smooth Sentences
Frank stared at the dirty walls as he stirred the paint. Knowing he had to wash the walls, he filled a bucket with water and special soap. He scrubbed hard until the walls were clean. Then he started to paint.

88 • Grade 6

Combine simple sentences using a compound verb.

Simple Sentences
Diego Rivera was a great muralist. He was from Mexico. He was a greatly respected artist.

Compound and Complex Sentences
Diego Rivera was a great muralist from Mexico whose work was greatly respected.

Use a variety of sentence beginnings.

Too Many Sentences Beginning the Same Way
Marisol was excited. Marisol was invited to the art opening. The art opening was at the museum. The museum normally only showed work by adults. The museum was having a special exhibit. The museum was featuring student artists' paintings and sculptures.

Varied Beginnings
Marisol was excited. She had been invited to the art opening at the museum. Normally, the museum only showed work by adults. This, however, was a special exhibit that featured the paintings and sculptures of student artists.

Use different sentence lengths.

Too Many Sentences of the Same Length
A llama is not a wild animal. Llamas are quite gentle. People often make pets of them. The llama is native to South America. Herds of llamas are kept by people in Peru and Bolivia. Llamas climb easily over rocky terrain. They make good pack animals in the mountains.

Varied Lengths
A llama is not a wild animal. In fact, llamas are quite gentle and people often make pets of them. The llama is native to South America, where people in Peru and Bolivia keep herds of them. Llamas climb easily over rocky terrain, and they make good pack animals in the mountains.

Sentence Fluency • 89

WRITING STRATEGY

Minilesson 75

Understanding Sentence Fluency

Common Core State Standards: W.6.4, W.6.5

Objective: Improve sentence fluency in writing.
Guiding Question: How do I make my writing easy to read?

Teach/Model

Have students read the definition and bulleted points. Explain that writing sentences all the same length can make writing sound choppy or stilted. Point out how the draft on p. 88 is improved by using sentence variety. Explain that using different sentence structures and lengths will help the writing flow more smoothly.

Practice/Apply

Have students read the second model on p. 88 and discuss how the Choppy Sentences draft was made better in the Smooth Sentences draft.

Minilesson 76

Creating Complex Sentences

Common Core State Standards: W.6.2c, W.6.4, W.6.5

Objective: Create complex sentences.
Guiding Question: How do I write complex sentences?

Teach/Model

Explain that one way to combine sentences is to make complex sentences, such as in the first example on p. 89. Point out the dependent clause in the model, and explain that this is a complex sentence.

Practice/Apply

Write several short sentences on the board, such as *Sam had a dog. The dog competed in races.* Have students rewrite them as a single sentence with a dependent clause, such as *Sam had a dog that competed in races.*

Conventions

Conventions

Conventions are rules for grammar, spelling, punctuation, and capitalization. When you edit your writing, you check for conventions.

Conventions

- Always review your writing for spelling mistakes, even if you've used a computer spell checker.
- Check for capitalization in proper nouns and at the beginning of sentences.
- Check for correct end punctuation and use of commas in compound and complex sentences.
- Identify and correct sentence fragments and run-ons.

Editing Checklist

Use an editing checklist to review your writing.

____ My writing has a clear introduction and conclusion.

____ My ideas are well organized.

____ My ideas are linked with words, phrases, and clauses.

____ I have made specific word choices.

____ I have checked for spelling mistakes.

____ I have checked for correct use of capitalization and punctuation.

____ I have included a variety of sentences.

____ I have indented each paragraph.

Irregular Verbs

The past and past participle forms of irregular verbs are not formed by adding –ed or –d. Make sure to use the correct form of the verb.

Wrong Way	Right Way
I rung the bell to wake everyone up.	I rang the bell to wake everyone up.
Have you ever drank coconut juice?	Have you ever drunk coconut juice?

Coordinating Conjunctions

Use a comma and a coordinating conjunction (for, and, nor, but, or, yet, so) to combine two simple sentences into one compound sentence.

Wrong Way	Right Way
She enjoyed the book, the book took her a long time to read.	She enjoyed the book, but it took her a long time to read.
Melissa came in first place, Lucy came in second place.	Melissa came in first place, and Lucy came in second place.

Double Negatives

No, not, never, nowhere, nothing, nobody, no one, neither, and barely are examples of negatives. Use only one negative in a sentence.

Wrong Way	Right Way
My friend Drew hadn't never seen snow before.	My friend Drew hadn't ever seen snow before.
He says there isn't no better place than the beach.	He says there is no better place than the beach.

Direct Quotations

A direct quotation tells a speaker's exact words. Use quotation marks and a comma to set off a direct quotation from the rest of a sentence.

Wrong Way	Right Way
Vlad cried out That's not the way to handle the cat!	Vlad cried out, "That's not the way to handle the cat!"
I wish I could fly above the trees, said the baby sparrow.	"I wish I could fly above the trees," said the baby sparrow.

Minilesson 77

Introducing Conventions

Common Core State Standard: W.6.5

Objective: Understand conventions.

Guiding Question: What rules do I follow when writing?

Teach/Model

Have students read the definition and bulleted points. Explain that conventions are rules about grammar, punctuation, spelling, and capitalization. Good writers consider these as they write or keep them in mind when they are editing.

Practice/Apply

Discuss the checklist on p. 90. Tell students that they can use this checklist when they edit to make sure their writing follows conventions. Suggest that students use the checklist to edit a piece of their writing.

Minilesson 78

Editing for Conventions

Common Core State Standard: W.6.5

Objective: Edit a piece for conventions.

Guiding Question: How do I follow writing conventions?

Teach/Model

Have students read the examples on p. 91. Point out that these are examples of common errors writers make. Walk them through each example and point out what makes the Right Way correct.

Practice/Apply

Write a few sentences with errors on the board, such as *There wasn't no snow this winter, I love snow said Dan.* Work with students to revise the sentences. (Example: *"There was no snow this winter, but I love snow," said Dan.*)

Writing Workshop

Writing Workshop

A **writing workshop** can help you get your revised draft ready to publish. In a writing workshop, you exchange your work with other students. They ask you questions and make suggestions to help you refine and edit your work. You do the same for them.

Asking Questions

- As you read your classmates' work, note any ideas you would like to know more about. Ask for clarification on those points.
- Do a quick check of capitalization, punctuation, spelling, and grammar. Sometimes it is easier for a new reader to find errors than for the writer to do so.
- Be polite! It can be hard to have your work criticized, so ask questions and offer suggestions in a constructive way.

Tapping the Earth

We have to find a way to heat and cool our homes without using gas or oil. In fact, we already have — it's called geothermal heating and cooling. It uses pumps to bring the heat of the earth into homes in cold weather. It also uses the cooler temperatures of the earth to cool the indoors in hot weather. Many countries, such as Iceland, New zealand, and Turkey, already use geothermal systems for a lot of their heating and cooling. Unfortunately, it costs a lot to set up the system, but over time, lower utility bills will pay for it. In fact, homeowners would save between 30 percent and 70 percent of his total utility costs!

Peer Questions
- Can you define "geothermal"?
- Do you know how much it costs to set up a geothermal system?
- Can you tell more about where geothermal heating and cooling can be used?
- Are the names of the countries all spelled and capitalized correctly?
- Are your grammar and punctuation correct?

Another way to use a writing workshop is to collaborate. When you collaborate, you and other classmates work together to write one piece.

Collaboration

- Share ideas. Open your mind to new opinions.
- Share tasks. Each person in the group plays a role in getting the job done.
- Think about what you do best. How can you best help your group reach its goal?
- Stay on task. Do not allow the discussion to fall apart.
- Make sure everyone remembers the group's goal and works towards it.

How to Collaborate

Choose a reasonable topic. Ask
- What is the assignment?
- What do we already know about the topic?
- What do we still need to find out about the topic?
- Who might want to read about the topic?

Make the right choices. Ask
- How can we make our writing clearer?
- Have we chosen the best words to use?
- Do we need to add or cut any information?

Remember your chosen goal. Ask
- How do we feel about the finished work?
- Does it say everything we want it to say?
- Does it fulfill the assignment?

Minilesson 79

Understanding the Writing Workshop

Common Core State Standard: W.6.5

Objective: Understand how a writing workshop functions.

Guiding Question: How can a writing workshop help me improve my writing?

Teach/Model

Ask students to read p. 92. Point out that the purpose of a writing workshop is to suggest how a piece of writing can be polished. Explain that students asked the questions in the Peer Questions box after reading a classmate's paragraph.

Practice/Apply

Have students discuss how the peer questions will help the writer clarify information and correct errors in "Tapping the Earth."

Minilesson 80

Collaborating with Classmates

Common Core State Standard: W.6.5

Objective: Collaborate with your classmates.

Guiding Question: How can I work with my classmates to write something?

Teach/Model

Have students read the definition and bulleted tips under Collaboration on p. 93. Then point out the How to Collaborate box. Tell students that they can use these questions to guide their collaboration.

Practice/Apply

Divide the class into groups. Have them use the tips and questions on p. 93 to collaborate on a short piece of writing about solar power, wind power, or another form of energy.

Using the Internet

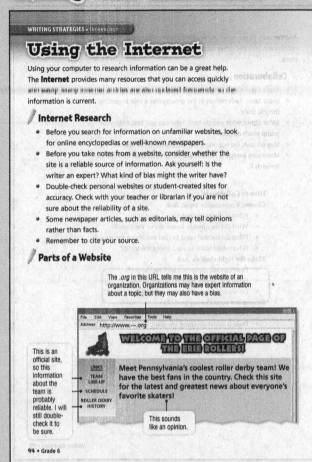

WRITING STRATEGIES • TECHNOLOGY

Using the Internet

Using your computer to research information can be a great help. The **Internet** provides many resources that you can access quickly and easily. Many Internet articles are also updated frequently, so the information is current.

Internet Research

- Before you search for information on unfamiliar websites, look for online encyclopedias or well-known newspapers.
- Before you take notes from a website, consider whether the site is a reliable source of information. Ask yourself: Is the writer an expert? What kind of bias might the writer have?
- Double-check personal websites or student-created sites for accuracy. Check with your teacher or librarian if you are not sure about the reliability of a site.
- Some newspaper articles, such as editorials, may tell opinions rather than facts.
- Remember to cite your source.

Parts of a Website

The *.org* in this URL tells me this is the website of an organization. Organizations may have expert information about a topic, but they may also have a bias.

This is an official site, so this information about the team is probably reliable. I will still double-check it to be sure.

WELCOME TO THE OFFICIAL PAGE OF THE ERIE ROLLERS!

Meet Pennsylvania's coolest roller derby team! We have the best fans in the country. Check this site for the latest and greatest news about everyone's favorite skaters!

This sounds like an opinion.

94 • Grade 6

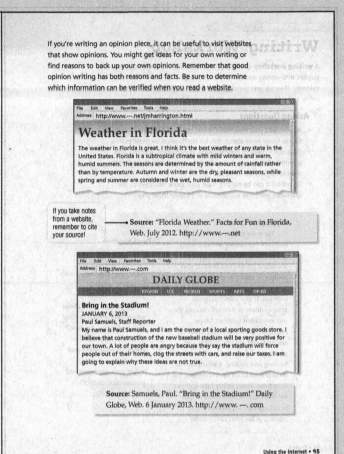

If you're writing an opinion piece, it can be useful to visit websites that show opinions. You might get ideas for your own writing or find reasons to back up your own opinions. Remember that good opinion writing has both reasons and facts. Be sure to determine which information can be verified when you read a website.

Weather in Florida

The weather in Florida is great. I think it's the best weather of any state in the United States. Florida is a subtropical climate with mild winters and warm, humid summers. The seasons are determined by the amount of rainfall rather than by temperature. Autumn and winter are the dry, pleasant seasons, while spring and summer are considered the wet, humid seasons.

If you take notes from a website, remember to cite your source!

Source: "Florida Weather." Facts for Fun in Florida, Web. July 2012. http://www.---.net

DAILY GLOBE

REGION   U.S.   WORLD   SPORTS   ARTS   OP-ED

Bring in the Stadium!
JANUARY 6, 2013
Paul Samuels, Staff Reporter
My name is Paul Samuels, and I am the owner of a local sporting goods store. I believe that construction of the new baseball stadium will be very positive for our town. A lot of people are angry because they say the stadium will force people out of their homes, clog the streets with cars, and raise our taxes. I am going to explain why these ideas are not true.

Source: Samuels, Paul. "Bring in the Stadium!" Daily Globe, Web. 6 January 2013. http://www. ---. com

Using the Internet • 95

Minilesson 81	Minilesson 82

Using the Internet

Common Core State Standard: W.6.8

Objective: Use the Internet to research information.

Guiding Question: How do I use the Internet to research information for my writing?

Teach/Model

Have students read p. 94. Explain that they can use the Internet to find encyclopedias and newspapers as well as websites like the one shown on this page.

Practice/Apply

Have students use a computer to find information about a favorite sports team, using websites and online encyclopedias and newspapers. Help them determine which sites are reliable sources.

Citing Websites

Common Core State Standard: W.6.8

Objective: Understand how to cite a website.

Guiding Question: How do I cite a website as a source of information for my writing?

Teach/Model

Tell students to study the two examples of websites on p. 95. Discuss how these sources of information are cited.

Practice/Apply

Have students use a computer to find two or three websites about your community or state. Guide them to cite each of these sources correctly, following the formats shown on p. 95.

Writing for the Web

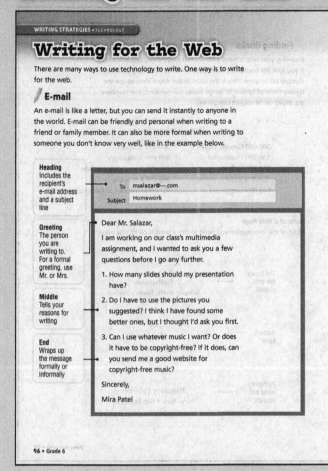

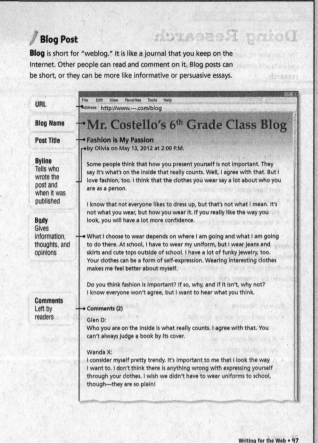

Minilesson 83

Writing a Formal E-mail

Common Core State Standard: W.6.6

Objective: Understand how to write a formal e-mail.

Guiding Question: How do I write a formal e-mail to someone I don't know very well?

Teach/Model

Have students read p. 96. Explain that the example on this page is an e-mail Mira Patel wrote to a teacher, Mr. Salazar, about a class assignment. Referring to the callouts, discuss the format of a formal e-mail.

Practice/Apply

Have students use a computer to compose an e-mail to someone they don't know very well. (You may decide whether the students will actually send the e-mails.) Remind them to use formal language and correct e-mail format.

Minilesson 84

Writing a Blog Post

Common Core State Standard: W.6.6

Objective: Understand how to write a blog post.

Guiding Question: What are the key parts of a blog post?

Teach/Model

With students, read p. 97. Explain that the example on this page shows the parts of a blog post. Ask *What is the title of the blog? What is the title of the post? Who wrote the post? What is the post about?*

Practice/Apply

Help students use a computer to create a blog post about their class. (It will not necessarily be published online.) Tell them to create a blog name and a post title. Remind them to include a byline and to tell information or share thoughts and opinions in the body.

Doing Research

Doing Research

The best way to support your informative or persuasive writing is to use facts and details. The best way to find facts and details is to do **research**.

Evaluating Sources

Sources are where you get your information. These include books, encyclopedias, periodicals, websites, and videos. Some sources are more reliable than others. How can you tell which sources are good? When looking at a new source, ask yourself these questions:

- Is the source published by experts in the field?
- If it is a website, is it trustworthy? *(Sites with .edu, .org, or .gov are educational, nonprofit, or government websites and can have good information.)*
- Is the source up-to-date? (It's important to have current facts, especially about science or current events.)
- Is the source relevant? Does it relate to your subject?

Primary vs. Secondary Sources

A primary source is first-hand information, usually from an eyewitness to an event. A secondary source includes information gathered by someone else. Here are some examples:

Primary Sources	Secondary Sources
• An interview with a scientist who studies earthquakes	• A newspaper article about the earthquake
• A journal entry by an earthquake survivor	• An encyclopedia entry about earthquakes
• A survey of people who witnessed the earthquake	• A TV documentary about the earthquake

Finding Books

Knowing your way around a library will make doing research easier. If you look for books in a library, you'll notice that every book has a number on its spine. This is the call number. Most libraries use the Dewey Decimal System to assign books call numbers. The numbers are based on 10 subject categories.

Dewey Decimal System

000–099 General Works	500–599 Sciences
100–199 Philosophy	600–699 Technology
200–299 Religion	700–799 Arts and Recreation
300–399 Social Sciences	800–899 Literature
400–499 Languages	900–999 History and Geography

Parts of a Title Page

Most of the information you need to cite a book is on its title page.

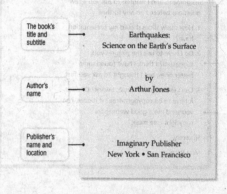

The book's title and subtitle → Earthquakes: Science on the Earth's Surface

Author's name → by Arthur Jones

Publisher's name and location → Imaginary Publisher New York • San Francisco

---

WRITING STRATEGY

Minilesson 85

Finding Reliable Sources

Common Core State Standard: W.6.8

Objective: Decide whether sources of information are reliable.

Guiding Question: How can I tell whether a source is good?

Teach/Model

Ask students to read p. 98. Explain that the bulleted questions under Evaluating Sources can help them determine whether a particular source is good.

Practice/Apply

Provide students with articles, eyewitness accounts, videos, interviews, and other sources about the same topic. Help them distinguish between primary and secondary sources. Then have students discuss how they can evaluate each source to decide if it is reliable.

Minilesson 86

Finding Books in a Library

Common Core State Standard: W.6.8

Objective: Find books in a library.

Guiding Question: How do I find the books I need when I do research in a library?

Teach/Model

Have students read p. 99. Explain that one way to find books in a library is by using the Dewey Decimal System. For example, a student doing research on skateboarding might look where books with the subject category 700–799 Arts and Recreation are shelved.

Practice/Apply

Bring books from your school or public library to class. Have students use call numbers and the chart on p. 99 to identify the subject category of each book.

Notetaking

Notetaking

When you gather information for a report or essay, you have to decide what information to include and how to organize it. As you research, take **notes** on note cards.

Note Cards

- Write a research question at the top of each card.
- You can write the answer by paraphrasing what the source says in your own words, copying a direct quote from the source, or writing a list with details from the source.
- Write the complete citation at the bottom of the card.

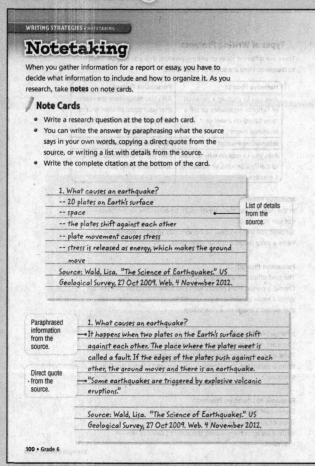

1. What causes an earthquake?
-- 20 plates on Earth's surface
-- space
-- the plates shift against each other
-- plate movement causes stress
-- stress is released as energy, which makes the ground move

Source: Wald, Lisa. "The Science of Earthquakes." US Geological Survey, 27 Oct 2009. Web. 4 November 2012.

List of details from the source.

Paraphrased information from the source.

1. What causes an earthquake?
It happens when two plates on the Earth's surface shift against each other. The place where the plates meet is called a fault. If the edges of the plates push against each other, the ground moves and there is an earthquake.

Direct quote from the source.

"Some earthquakes are triggered by explosive volcanic eruptions."

Source: Wald, Lisa. "The Science of Earthquakes." US Geological Survey, 27 Oct 2009. Web. 4 November 2012.

Keeping a Journal

Keeping a journal is another way to help with your notetaking. In a journal, you can express ideas, questions, thoughts, and feelings. This can help you later with your writing when you need to add to your main points or express your point of view.

Taking Notes in a Journal

- One way to take notes is to make two columns. Label one with the title of the text. Label the other Feelings and Responses.
- Read the text. In the left column, jot down quotations, ideas, and examples that confuse you, inspire you, or leave you asking questions. Include page numbers to refer back to the text.
- In the right column, jot down notes about the text. Include your feelings, thoughts, and any connections to the text you may have.

Robotics by Helena Domaine	Feelings and Responses
"These mechanical adventurers have computer brains that don't feel fear or panic." (634)	Ooh — this is some really strong language! It sets an exciting tone for the rest of the article.
"The science team had to call in a helicopter to rescue the robot." (635)	A helicopter? That sounds expensive.
"The Rovers also have a 'survival instinct' programmed into them." (636)	What's this "survival instinct"? I'd like to know more about this.
"The Swedish micro-bots are smaller than the hyphen between micro and bots in this sentence." (637)	Great description! I wonder what else can be that small.
-in 2003, robot soccer game at Carnegie Mellon University (638)	I would love to see this. Are there any games near my house?
-Bertram, robot butler (639)	This sounds funny. It reminds me of that old TV show.

Minilesson 87

Using Note Cards

Common Core State Standard: W.6.8

Objective: Understand how to take notes on note cards.

Guiding Question: How do I take notes on note cards when I research information for a report or an essay?

Teach/Model

Have students read p. 100. Explain that the examples on this page show how students used note cards to gather information about what causes an earthquake. Point out that the first card lists details and the second card paraphrases and directly quotes information.

Practice/Apply

Have students research what causes a volcano. Have them take notes, using the note card formats shown on p. 100. Remind students to properly cite the source.

Minilesson 88

Keeping a Journal

Common Core State Standard: W.6.8

Objective: Understand how to take notes in a journal.

Guiding Question: How will taking notes in a journal help me with my writing?

Teach/Model

Ask students to read p. 101. Explain that they can use a journal to take notes about a text as they read. Point out how a student did this while reading *Robotics* by Helena Domaine.

Practice/Apply

Have students review what the student wrote in the columns of the sample journal. Discuss how this student might use these quotations, ideas, questions, and feelings in his or her writing.

Writing to a Prompt

Writing to a Prompt

Sometimes your teacher may give a timed writing assignment for a class exercise or a test. You will be given a **prompt** that asks you a question or tells you what to write about.

Writing to a Prompt

- Look for key words that tell you what to do, such as explain, compare and contrast, convince or persuade, and summarize.
- Choose a focus, or main idea, for your writing.
- List and organize all your other ideas. Then add details, reasons, or facts to support your main idea.
- Spend about one-fourth of your time prewriting, half of your time drafting, and one-fourth of your time revising.

Sample Prompt:
Lewis and Clark's expedition to the West changed the United States. Think about how their expedition changed the United States. Write an essay explaining how their expedition changed the course of history in the United States.

Plan

My focus: Lewis and Clark opened the American West when they traveled to the Pacific Ocean.

- mapped a new route
- drew plants, animals, rocks
- created friendly relations with Native Americans

Draft
The westward expedition headed by Meriwether Lewis and William Clark opened up the land and the resources of the West to the whole country. Between 1803 and 1806, Lewis and Clark traveled from Pittsburgh to the Pacific Ocean. Their aims were to plan a route and report on what they saw along the way. They mapped a route across the country. In addition, they described and drew plants, animals, and geologic formations that they saw. Most important, they created friendly relations with Native Americans, which helped later groups to make the same trip more safely.

Types of Writing Prompts

There are different types of writing prompts that you may be asked to complete. Here are some of those types:

Narrative Prompt	Persuasive Prompt
Asks you to recount a personal or fictional experience or tell a story based on a real or imagined event	Asks you to convince the reader that your point of view is valid or that the reader should take a specific action
Informative Prompt	Response to Literature
Asks you to explain why or how, to clarify a process, or to define a concept	Asks you to answer questions about something you read

Narrative Prompt:
In the near future, space travel might be accessible for everyone—not just astronauts.
Suppose you were to have an opportunity to travel into space.
Write a story describing your experience.

Persuasive Prompt:
The post office honors people by putting them on stamps.
Choose a person from history who you think should be on a stamp.
Write a letter to persuade the United States Postal Service to use that person's image on a new stamp.

Informative Prompt:
There are many environmental issues that cause concern.
Think of an environmental issue that concerns you.
Write a paragraph that describes the issue and offers a possible solution.

Response to Literature Prompt:
Every novel shows an author's point of view.
Think of your favorite novel.
Write a paragraph explaining the author's point of view in this novel.

WRITING STRATEGY

Minilesson 89

Introducing Prompts

Common Core State Standards: W.6.4, W.6.10

Objective: Understand how to write to a prompt.

Guiding Question: How do I write to a prompt?

Teach/Model

Instruct students to read p. 102. Explain that the example on this page shows how a student wrote to a prompt, using a graphic organizer to plan an essay about how Lewis and Clark's expedition changed the course of history in the United States.

Practice/Apply

Have students discuss the prompt and the student writer's response. Ask *What key word in the prompt tells what to do? What is the main idea of the student's essay? What details, reasons, or facts support the main idea?*

Minilesson 90

Understanding Different Kinds of Prompts

Common Core State Standards: W.6.4, W.6.10

Objective: Understand four different types of prompts.

Guiding Question: How do I respond to different types of prompts?

Teach/Model

Have students read p. 103. Point out that the chart shows four types of prompts: narrative, persuasive, informative, and response to literature. Explain that specific examples of each prompt follow the chart.

Practice/Apply

Have students use the bulleted tips on p. 102 to write a response to one of the prompts given on this page.

Checklists and Rubrics

Checklists and Rubrics

Use this rubric to evaluate your writing. Circle a number in each column to rate your writing. Then revise your writing to improve your score.

	• Focus • Support	• Organization
Score 6	My writing is focused and supported by facts or details.	My writing has a clear introduction and conclusion. Ideas are clearly organized.
Score 5	My writing is mostly focused and supported by facts or details.	My writing has an introduction and a conclusion. Ideas are mostly organized.
Score 4	My writing is mostly focused and supported by some facts or details.	My writing has an introduction and a conclusion. Most ideas are organized.
Score 3	Some of my writing is focused and supported by some facts or details.	My writing has an introduction or a conclusion but might be missing one. Some ideas are organized.
Score 2	My writing is not focused and is supported by few facts or details.	My writing might not have an introduction or a conclusion. Few ideas are organized.
Score 1	My writing is not focused or supported by facts or details.	My writing is missing an introduction and a conclusion. Few or no ideas are organized.

	• Word Choice • Voice	• Conventions • Sentence Fluency
	Ideas are linked with words, phrases, and clauses. Words are specific. My voice connects with the reader in a unique way.	My writing has no errors in spelling, grammar, capitalization, or punctuation. There are a variety of sentences.
	Most ideas are linked with words, phrases, and clauses. Words are specific. My voice connects with the reader.	My writing has few errors in spelling, grammar, capitalization, or punctuation. There is some variety of sentences.
	Some ideas are linked with words, phrases, and clauses. Some words are specific. My voice connects with the reader.	My writing has some errors in spelling, grammar, capitalization, or punctuation. There is some variety of sentences.
	Some ideas are linked with words, phrases, or clauses. Few words are specific. My voice may connect with the reader.	My writing has some errors in spelling, grammar, capitalization, or punctuation. There is little variety of sentences.
	Ideas may be linked with words, phrases, or clauses. Few words are specific. My voice may connect with the reader.	My writing has many errors in spelling, grammar, capitalization, or punctuation. There is little variety of sentences. Some sentences are incomplete.
	Ideas may not be linked with words, phrases, or clauses. No words are specific. My voice does not connect with the reader.	My writing has many errors in spelling, grammar, capitalization, or punctuation. There is no variety of sentences. Sentences are incomplete.

WRITING STRATEGY

Minilesson 91

Introducing Rubrics

Common Core State Standard: W.6.5

Objective: Understand what a rubric is and how it is organized.

Guiding Question: What is a rubric, and how is it organized?

Teach/Model

Instruct students to read pp. 104–105. Point out that the rubric on these pages is a chart with four headings across the top and a numbered scoring guide down the left side. Tell students that they can use a rubric to evaluate how well a piece of their own writing fulfills each listed trait or characteristic.

Practice/Apply

Have students identify and discuss the writing traits in the rubric headings. Have them locate the pages in the handbook that explain each of the traits.

Minilesson 92

Using a Rubric to Improve Writing

Common Core State Standard: W.6.5

Objective: Use a rubric to improve a piece of writing.

Guiding Question: How can I use a rubric to improve my writing?

Teach/Model

Model how to use this rubric to assign a score to a given piece of writing. Tell students that they can use a rubric as a guide when prewriting, drafting, editing, or revising. A rubric offers feedback about what changes are needed.

Practice/Apply

Have students use this rubric to evaluate a piece of their own writing. Then have them revise their work to improve their score.

Cause-Effect Essay

Cause-Effect Essay

A **cause-effect essay** describes something that happened (the effect) and explains how a person, object, or event made it happen (the cause).

Parts of a Cause-Effect Essay

- A topic sentence that introduces a cause, an effect, or both
- Details that explain the causes
- Details that describe the effects
- Transition words or phrases that connect ideas
- An ending that ties together ideas

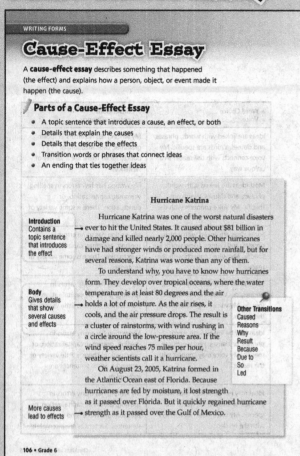

Hurricane Katrina

Introduction
Contains a topic sentence that introduces the effect

Hurricane Katrina was one of the worst natural disasters ever to hit the United States. It caused about $81 billion in damage and killed nearly 2,000 people. Other hurricanes have had stronger winds or produced more rainfall, but for several reasons, Katrina was worse than any of them.

Body
Gives details that show several causes and effects

To understand why, you have to know how hurricanes form. They develop over tropical oceans, where the water temperature is at least 80 degrees and the air holds a lot of moisture. As the air rises, it cools, and the air pressure drops. The result is a cluster of rainstorms, with wind rushing in a circle around the low-pressure area. If the wind speed reaches 75 miles per hour, weather scientists call it a hurricane.

Other Transitions
Caused
Reasons
Why
Result
Because
Due to
So
Led

On August 23, 2005, Katrina formed in the Atlantic Ocean east of Florida. Because hurricanes are fed by moisture, it lost strength as it passed over Florida. But it quickly regained hurricane strength as it passed over the Gulf of Mexico.

More causes lead to effects

These two paragraphs give details about the causes that led to the effects described.

The waters in the Gulf were unusually warm that year. The pressure of the atmosphere at the center of the storm was among the lowest ever recorded. Due to these conditions, wind speeds increased to over 175 miles per hour. These swirling winds caused the storm to double in size. By the time Katrina reached Louisiana, on the morning of August 29, it was one of the most powerful storms to hit the United States in the last 100 years.

The city of New Orleans, Louisiana, lay directly in the path of the hurricane. The storm dumped 8 to 15 inches of rain on parts of Louisiana. The wind and surging seas caused boats and cars to ram into buildings. In New Orleans, the storm caused Lake Pontchartrain to overflow. Before Katrina, a system of walls, called levees, was designed to hold back the waters. During the storm, many levees broke under the pressure of the water because they had been poorly built. In all, 53 levees in the New Orleans area failed, with the result that 80 percent of the city was underwater.

The floods caused thousands of people to be stranded for days without food or clean water. Many of them took shelter in a football stadium, but others were trapped on roofs, and many drowned. There was plenty of warning about the storm, but roads became clogged with traffic, so cars could not move. In the days after the storm, the Coast Guard rescued about 33,500 people. The U.S. government, other states, private charities, and even other countries sent aid. A lot of blame went around for the slow response to the storm and for the poorly built levees.

Ending
Shows the final effect and wraps up the ideas of the essay

We can't control nature. But Hurricane Katrina led the country to resolve to be better prepared for natural disasters.

WRITING MODELS AND FORMS

Minilesson 93

Understanding the Cause-Effect Essay

Common Core State Standard: W.6.2

Objective: Understand how to use the information presented about the cause-effect essay.

Guiding Question: How can I use these pages to help me write a good cause-effect essay?

Teach/Model

Have students read the definition and bulleted points. Add that the opening statement can introduce the cause, the effect, or both. Have the students read the model. Point out details about the cause.

Practice/Apply

Have students use their own words to list the causes and effects.

Minilesson 94

Connecting Your Ideas

Common Core State Standard: W.6.2

Objective: Use transition words to connect your ideas in a cause-effect essay.

Guiding Question: How do I connect my ideas in a cause-effect essay?

Teach/Model

Explain to students that the writer connected the ideas in each paragraph using transition words and phrases specific to a cause-effect essay, such as *result, because,* and *due to.*

Practice/Apply

Have students find and underline the transition words and phrases in the text. Discuss how they connect the ideas in the essay.

Problem-Solution Essay

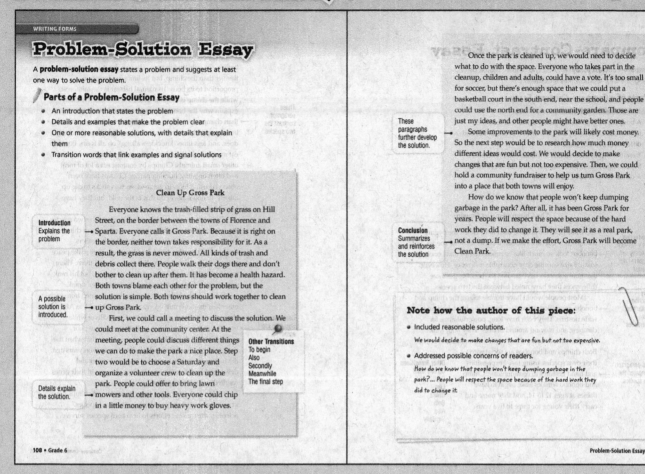

Problem-Solution Essay

A **problem-solution essay** states a problem and suggests at least one way to solve the problem.

Parts of a Problem-Solution Essay

- An introduction that states the problem
- Details and examples that make the problem clear
- One or more reasonable solutions, with details that explain them
- Transition words that link examples and signal solutions

Clean Up Gross Park

Introduction Explains the problem

Everyone knows the trash-filled strip of grass on Hill Street, on the border between the towns of Florence and Sparta. Everyone calls it Gross Park. Because it is right on the border, neither town takes responsibility for it. As a result, the grass is never mowed. All kinds of trash and debris collect there. People walk their dogs there and don't bother to clean up after them. It has become a health hazard. Both towns blame each other for the problem, but the solution is simple. Both towns should work together to clean up Gross Park.

A possible solution is introduced.

First, we could call a meeting to discuss the solution. We could meet at the community center. At the meeting, people could discuss different things we can do to make the park a nice place. Step two would be to choose a Saturday and organize a volunteer crew to clean up the park. People could offer to bring lawn mowers and other tools. Everyone could chip in a little money to buy heavy work gloves.

Details explain the solution.

Other Transitions
To begin
Also
Secondly
Meanwhile
The final step

Once the park is cleaned up, we would need to decide what to do with the space. Everyone who takes part in the cleanup, children and adults, could have a vote. It's too small for soccer, but there's enough space that we could put a basketball court in the south end, near the school, and people could use the north end for a community garden. Those are just my ideas, and other people might have better ones.

These paragraphs further develop the solution.

Some improvements to the park will likely cost money. So the next step would be to research how much money different ideas would cost. We would decide to make changes that are fun but not too expensive. Then, we could hold a community fundraiser to help us turn Gross Park into a place that both towns will enjoy.

Conclusion Summarizes and reinforces the solution

How do we know that people won't keep dumping garbage in the park? After all, it has been Gross Park for years. People will respect the space because of the hard work they did to change it. They will see it as a real park, not a dump. If we make the effort, Gross Park will become Clean Park.

Note how the author of this piece:

- Included reasonable solutions.
  We would decide to make changes that are fun but not too expensive.
- Addressed possible concerns of readers.
  How do we know that people won't keep dumping garbage in the park?... People will respect the space because of the hard work they did to change it.

WRITING MODELS AND FORMS

Minilesson 95

Understanding the Problem-Solution Essay

Common Core State Standard: W.6.2

Objective: Understand how to use the information presented about the problem-solution essay.

Guiding Question: How can I use these pages to help me write a good problem-solution essay?

Teach/Model

Have students read the definition and bulleted points. Point out that the writer explains the problem and gives reasonable solutions. Read the model together. Point out that the conclusion reinforces the solution and addresses possible concerns of the reader.

Practice/Apply

Have students underline the solution in the introduction and then underline supporting details in the body of the essay.

Minilesson 96

Explaining the Solution

Common Core State Standard: W.6.2

Objective: Develop a solution to a problem using details to explain the solution.

Guiding Question: How do I use details to explain the solution to a problem?

Teach/Model

Mention to students that the writer introduced the solution and then gave details to explain it. Point out that the details explain each step of the solution in a logical order.

Practice/Apply

Have students write a heading for each body paragraph and list each paragraph's details in numbered steps. Discuss how the headings and details clearly explain the solution.

Writing for Common Core • **91**

Compare-Contrast Essay

Compare-Contrast Essay

A **compare-contrast essay** tells how two or more people, places, or things are alike and how they are different.

Parts of a Compare-Contrast Essay

- An introduction that states the main idea
- A body that is organized logically: similarities first, then differences; differences, then similarities; or similarities and differences point by point
- Transition words that indicate similarities and differences
- Supporting sentences that explain similarities and differences
- A conclusion that sums up the essay

The Chimp's Smaller Cousin

Introduction
Tells what topic the essay will compare and contrast

Body
Describes similarities, then differences

This paragraph compares the two species.

Until 1954, the bonobo used to be called the pygmy chimpanzee. Scientists labeled them as separate species, but bonobos look so much like common chimps that bonobos' smaller size was the only noticeable difference. However, the more scientists have studied the bonobo, the more differences other have noted between the two species.

Most people would have trouble telling the chimp and bonobo apart. Both have dark faces, long black hair, and wide nostrils. They both have long, powerful arms for climbing and moving around in trees. They both walk upright when carrying things with their hands and arms. Both chimps and bonobos are social with their own species, using facial expressions and hand gestures to communicate. Chimp and bonobo females alike begin to have babies at ages 12 to 14, and they nurse and carry their young for three to five years.

Other Transitions
On one hand
On the other hand
Like
Unlike
Both
Also
Similarly

These paragraphs contrast the two species.

The differences between the species show themselves both in the wild and in zoos. The bonobo is shorter and thinner than the chimp, but its limbs are longer in proportion to its body. Its natural habitat is the rainforest, while the chimp is at home in several habitats. That may explain why the bonobo spends more of its time in trees than chimps do, even in zoos. When it is on the ground, the bonobo spends more time walking upright than the chimp does, and less time "knuckle-walking" on all fours. Bonobos eat mostly fruit, though sometimes they hunt monkeys and other small animals. Chimps by contrast eat a lot of meat and often organize hunting parties. Chimps have been observed using tools to get food, such as sticks to dig up insects. Bonobos never do this in the wild, but they have learned how to do it in zoos.

There are also social differences between the two species. An "alpha male" usually controls a community of chimps. He makes himself the boss by threatening the others. Females, on the other hand, lead bonobos. They make peace among the males and form alliances to control them. There may be an alpha male in a bonobo community, but his rank among other males is determined by his mother's rank.

Conclusion
Sums up the essay

Scientists think that the two species separated from each other less than one million years ago. In the wild, in Africa, chimpanzees only live north of the Congo River while bonobos live south of the river. Both species are poor swimmers and don't like to swim. It is likely that when the river formed, about one and a half to two million years ago, the two groups were separated from each other and developed in different ways. In time, changes in their genes resulted in separate species.

Unfortunately, one last thing bonobos and chimps have in common is that they are both endangered species. Scientists are making efforts to help both species survive.

WRITING MODELS AND FORMS

Minilesson 97

Understanding the Compare-Contrast Essay

Common Core State Standard: W.6.2

Objective: Understand how to use the information presented about the compare-contrast essay.

Guiding Question: How can I use these pages to help me write a good compare-contrast essay?

Teach/Model

Have students read the definition and bulleted points on p. 110. Have them read the model. Point out that the transition words can show comparisons or contrasts.

Practice/Apply

Have students underline the main ideas in the introduction and label them "similarity" or "difference."

Minilesson 98

Explaining Similarities and Differences

Common Core State Standard: W.6.2

Objective: Explain similarities and differences using supporting sentences.

Guiding Question: How do I use supporting sentences to explain similarities and differences?

Teach/Model

Tell students that the writer uses one paragraph to explain similarities, point by point, and then contrasts the two subjects using three paragraphs to explain differences with supporting details.

Practice/Apply

Have students underline the main idea of each body paragraph and number the supporting details.

How-to Essay

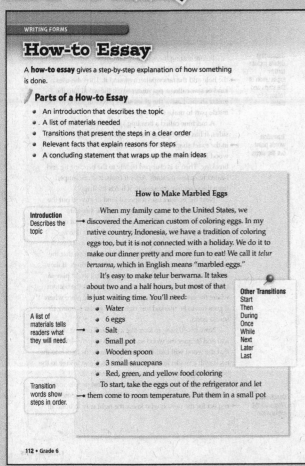

How-to Essay

A **how-to essay** gives a step-by-step explanation of how something is done.

Parts of a How-to Essay

- An introduction that describes the topic
- A list of materials needed
- Transitions that present the steps in a clear order
- Relevant facts that explain reasons for steps
- A concluding statement that wraps up the main ideas

How to Make Marbled Eggs

Introduction
Describes the topic

When my family came to the United States, we discovered the American custom of coloring eggs. In my native country, Indonesia, we have a tradition of coloring eggs too, but it is not connected with a holiday. We do it to make our dinner pretty and more fun to eat! We call it *telur berwarna*, which in English means "marbled eggs."

It's easy to make telur berwarna. It takes about two and a half hours, but most of that is just waiting time. You'll need:

A list of materials tells readers what they will need.

- Water
- 6 eggs
- Salt
- Small pot
- Wooden spoon
- 3 small saucepans
- Red, green, and yellow food coloring

Other Transitions
Start
Then
During
Once
While
Next
Later
Last

Transition words show steps in order.

To start, take the eggs out of the refrigerator and let them come to room temperature. Put them in a small pot

carefully so that you don't crack the shells. Cover with cold water and add salt. Then heat the water gently—don't let it boil! During the first five minutes, keep stirring with the handle of a wooden spoon to make sure the yolks stay in the middle.

Body
Explains steps in the process as well as reasons for the steps

Once the water is bubbling gently, cook for about seven more minutes. Then remove the pot from the stove. Carefully pour the hot water into the sink. Then quickly run cold water over the eggs. This is to make sure the eggs don't stick to the insides of the shells.

While the eggs are cooling, fill three small saucepans with water and add food coloring, one color to each. Put in enough food coloring to give the water a deep, rich color. Then bring the saucepans to a heavy boil.

Next, tap each egg on a hard surface. This is the tricky step. You want to tap hard enough to crack the shells, but not hard enough to break off any part of them. Using the wooden spoon, put two eggs in each of the saucepans and simmer for another five minutes. Then turn off the heat and allow the eggs to cool in the colored water for at least two hours.

Later, peel the eggs. They should have a bright, marbled color. The last step is the best: Serve the eggs and eat them! They taste just like regular hard-boiled eggs, but they're prettier and more fun to eat.

Conclusion
Suggests some uses for the finished product

In Indonesia, we usually serve telur berwarna cut in halves on top of sticky yellow rice seasoned with fried onion, coconut, and spices. But you can serve it lots of different ways. Try it on top of a green salad, or turn it into an egg-salad sandwich. If you bring it to school in your lunchbox, though, be warned that your friends will want to trade for it!

WRITING MODELS AND FORMS

Minilesson 99

Understanding the How-to Essay

Common Core State Standard: W.6.2

Objective: Understand how to use the information presented about the how-to essay.

Guiding Question: How can I use these pages to help me write a good how-to essay?

Teach/Model

Have students read the definition and bulleted points on p. 112. Add that the essay explains why each step in a process is done. Have the students read the model. Point out that the transition words show the order in which the steps should be done.

Practice/Apply

Have students underline the transition words and rewrite the steps as a numbered list.

Minilesson 100

Explaining the Steps

Common Core State Standard: W.6.2

Objective: Explain reasons for the steps with relevant facts.

Guiding Question: How do I explain the steps in my how-to essay?

Teach/Model

Explain to students that the writer introduced the topic, listed the materials, and then explained each step of the project, giving detailed reasons for each step. Each paragraph provides relevant facts to explain each step of the process.

Practice/Apply

Have students underline steps and circle any relevant facts that explain each step. Have them connect the circled facts with an arrow pointing to the relevant step.

Writing for Common Core • **93**

Explanation Essay

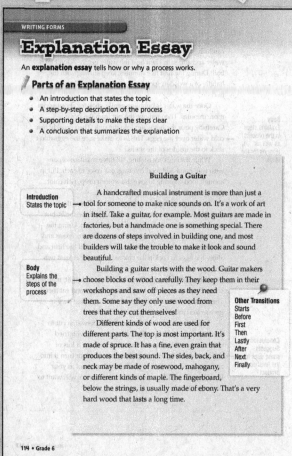

Explanation Essay

An **explanation essay** tells how or why a process works.

Parts of an Explanation Essay
- An introduction that states the topic
- A step-by-step description of the process
- Supporting details to make the steps clear
- A conclusion that summarizes the explanation

Building a Guitar

Introduction
States the topic

A handcrafted musical instrument is more than just a tool for someone to make nice sounds on. It's a work of art in itself. Take a guitar, for example. Most guitars are made in factories, but a handmade one is something special. There are dozens of steps involved in building one, and most builders will take the trouble to make it look and sound beautiful.

Body
Explains the steps of the process

Building a guitar starts with the wood. Guitar makers choose blocks of wood carefully. They keep them in their workshops and saw off pieces as they need them. Some say they only use wood from trees that they cut themselves!

Different kinds of wood are used for different parts. The top is most important. It's made of spruce. It has a fine, even grain that produces the best sound. The sides, back, and neck may be made of rosewood, mahogany, or different kinds of maple. The fingerboard, below the strings, is usually made of ebony. That's a very hard wood that lasts a long time.

Other Transitions
Starts
Before
First
Then
Lastly
After
Next
Finally

Supporting details include further explanation of the steps and reasons for them.

Before cutting the top, the guitar maker first marks off the round hole in the middle. She uses special tools to cut the hole and the fancy pattern around it. Then she uses a kind of saw called a pin router to cut the wood into the guitar shape. Lastly, she glues small pieces of wood to the inside part to make it stronger.

Transition words point out the steps.

A machine called a bending jig is used to shape the sides. It has a metal part that is heated by electricity and is in the exact shape of the side of a guitar. First, a strip of wood is soaked in hot water so that it will bend without breaking. Then it is clamped tightly to the bending jig and heated for a few minutes. After it cools, it is unclamped from the machine. Amazingly, it holds its shape.

Next the builder uses a special kind of glue to put the top, sides, and back together. So far, all the steps are something that any skilled carpenter could do. But now comes the part that turns these pieces of wood into a musical instrument. The builder cuts grooves in the neck where the frets will go. Those are the metal strips that the guitar player's fingers will hold against the strings. If they are not in exactly the right places, the guitar won't play in tune! The same goes for the bridge, the strip at the bottom where the ends of the strings are fastened. The place where it goes has to be marked just right if the guitar is going to sound good.

Now it's starting to look like a guitar. The next step is to seal and lacquer the wood so that it looks pretty—and so that the wood will last. The builder pounds the frets into the neck with a mallet and then glues the neck and bridge to the body. Finally, the pegs and strings are put in.

Conclusion
Wraps up the explanation

Now we're ready for some music! Most people admire a person who plays the guitar well. But let's have some respect for the person who knew the right way to build it!

WRITING MODELS AND FORMS

Minilesson 101

Understanding the Explanation Essay

Common Core State Standard: W.6.2

Objective: Understand how to use the information presented about the explanation essay.

Guiding Question: How can I use these pages to help me write a good explanation essay?

Teach/Model

Have students read the definition and bulleted points. Add that an explanation is like a how-to, but it can also explain how something is made or how something works. Have the students read the model. Add that transition words are used to show steps.

Practice/Apply

Have students underline the main topic and number the steps of the process explained in the essay.

Minilesson 102

Describing Step-by-Step

Common Core State Standard: W.6.2

Objective: Describe a process in logically organized steps.

Guiding Question: How do I explain a process step-by-step?

Teach/Model

Tell students that the writer explains how a process works by listing the steps of the process in order, using transition words to organize the steps. The writer also describes the steps with details and reasons for doing each step.

Practice/Apply

Have students write a brief explanation of a process they are familiar with, such as building a model airplane or getting ready for school. Guide them to use transitions and arrange steps in a logical order.

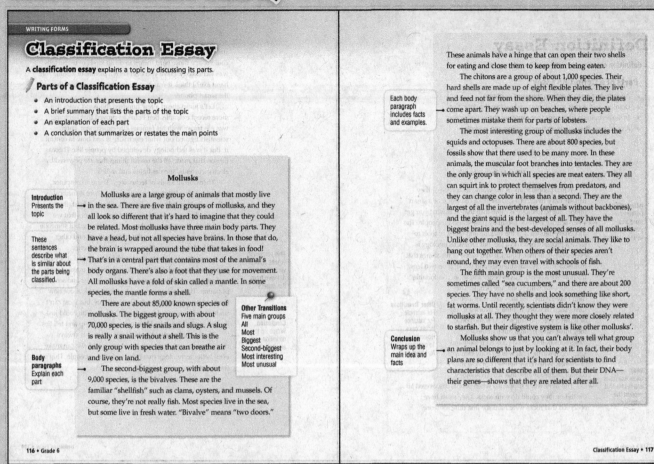

Classification Essay

WRITING FORMS

Classification Essay

A **classification essay** explains a topic by discussing its parts.

Parts of a Classification Essay

- An introduction that presents the topic
- A brief summary that lists the parts of the topic
- An explanation of each part
- A conclusion that summarizes or restates the main points

Mollusks

Introduction Presents the topic

Mollusks are a large group of animals that mostly live in the sea. There are five main groups of mollusks, and they all look so different that it's hard to imagine that they could be related. Most mollusks have three main body parts. They have a head, but not all species have brains. In those that do, the brain is wrapped around the tube that takes in food! That's in a central part that contains most of the animal's body organs. There's also a foot that they use for movement. All mollusks have a fold of skin called a mantle. In some species, the mantle forms a shell.

These sentences describe what is similar about the parts being classified.

There are about 85,000 known species of mollusks. The biggest group, with about 70,000 species, is the snails and slugs. A slug is really a snail without a shell. This is the only group with species that can breathe air and live on land.

Other Transitions
Five main groups
All
Most
Biggest
Second-biggest
Most interesting
Most unusual

Body paragraphs Explain each part

The second-biggest group, with about 9,000 species, is the bivalves. These are the familiar "shellfish" such as clams, oysters, and mussels. Of course, they're not really fish. Most species live in the sea, but some live in fresh water. "Bivalve" means "two doors."

116 • Grade 6

These animals have a hinge that can open their two shells for eating and close them to keep from being eaten.

The chitons are a group of about 1,000 species. Their hard shells are made up of eight flexible plates. They live and feed not far from the shore. When they die, the plates come apart. They wash up on beaches, where people sometimes mistake them for parts of lobsters.

Each body paragraph includes facts and examples.

The most interesting group of mollusks includes the squids and octopuses. There are about 800 species, but fossils show that there used to be many more. In these animals, the muscular foot branches into tentacles. They are the only group in which all species are meat eaters. They all can squirt ink to protect themselves from predators, and they can change color in less than a second. They are the largest of all the invertebrates (animals without backbones), and the giant squid is the largest of all. They have the biggest brains and the best-developed senses of all mollusks. Unlike other mollusks, they are social animals. They like to hang out together. When others of their species aren't around, they may even travel with schools of fish.

The fifth main group is the most unusual. They're sometimes called "sea cucumbers," and there are about 200 species. They have no shells and look something like short, fat worms. Until recently, scientists didn't know they were mollusks at all. They thought they were more closely related to starfish. But their digestive system is like other mollusks'.

Conclusion Wraps up the main idea and facts

Mollusks show us that you can't always tell what group an animal belongs to just by looking at it. In fact, their body plans are so different that it's hard for scientists to find characteristics that describe all of them. But their DNA—their genes—shows that they are related after all.

Classification Essay • 117

WRITING MODELS AND FORMS

Minilesson 103

Understanding the Classification Essay

Common Core State Standard: W.6.2

Objective: Understand how to use the information presented about the classification essay.

Guiding Question: How can I use these pages to help me write a classification essay?

Teach/Model

Have students read the definition and bulleted points on p. 116. Have students read the model. Note that the writer concludes with a paraphrase of the main idea stated in the introduction.

Practice/Apply

Have students underline the main idea in the introduction and in the conclusion. Ask them to restate the main idea in their own words.

Minilesson 104

Explaining Parts of a Topic

Common Core State Standard: W.6.2

Objective: Explain parts of a topic using facts and examples.

Guiding Question: How do I explain the parts of a topic?

Teach/Model

Tell students that the writer uses facts and examples to describe and explain parts of the topic. Each body paragraph describes a part of the topic, and the conclusion ties all of the facts together and restates the main idea.

Practice/Apply

Have students underline the part being described in each body paragraph. Ask students to say which detail or example in each paragraph gives them the clearest idea of what the part being described is like.

Writing for Common Core • 95

Definition Essay

WRITING FORMS

Definition Essay

A **definition essay** explains the meaning of a word or phrase.

Parts of a Definition Essay

- An introduction that defines the word or phrase
- Opinions and details that support and explain the definition
- Often an opinion statement that expresses the writer's views
- A conclusion that wraps up the definition and examples

What Is Technology?

Introduction
Defines the word and states the writer's opinion

When people think of the word "technology," they usually have in mind a gadget like a computer or a smart phone. But technology is more than that. It is what you get when science is made useful by people and for people. The dictionary defines it as the making and using of tools to solve a problem or to do a job. But I think technology is even more than that. I think that it is one of the things that makes us human, like language and walking on two legs. It's how we make our lives better and more comfortable.

Body
Gives examples and details that support the definition

Let's start with Stone Age people. They didn't invent fire. But they saw it all around them, such as when lightning struck a forest or when a volcano erupted. At some point, they must have figured out that the scary, dangerous flames could cook their food and keep them warm. That was an early example of science. When they figured out how to control and make fire, that was technology.

Other Transitions
For example
For instance
In this case
However
To conclude
As I have said

The same thing happened when people discovered all the things they could do with rocks. They must have observed that rocks were hard the first time someone stubbed his or her toe on one. But figuring out that they could shape those hard things to do all kinds of useful jobs was technology. Have you ever seen a picture of a Stone Age hand axe? I think it was a more important invention than the smart phone.

Let's jump ahead a few hundred thousand years to a more recent example. Ben Franklin proved that lightning was electricity with his famous kite experiment. Later, scientists figured out what electricity is and how to control it. But it was technology developed by people like Thomas Edison that made all the useful things that are powered by electric currents, such as lights and radios.

There are all kinds of technology. There is computer technology that helps us communicate. There is medical technology that helps save lives. Last but not least, there's simple technology like spoons and screwdrivers that we don't think about because they are so ordinary. But someone had to figure out how to make and use them, and other people had to figure out how to make them better.

This paragraph argues against views that are different from the writer's.

Some people seem to think technology is bad. They like to point out that a lot of technology goes into making more and more powerful weapons. They look at cars and see pollution. They look at new machines and talk about how they put people out of work. That's all true, but I just can't understand how people can think that way. You could just as well say talking is bad because people gossip and tell lies.

Conclusion
Wraps up the definition and examples

The best thing about technology is that it is always changing. As we learn more about the world, we can make even better technology that helps even more people. That's the human way.

WRITING MODELS AND FORMS

Minilesson 105

Understanding the Definition Essay

Common Core State Standard: W.6.2

Objective: Understand how to use the information presented about the definition essay.

Guiding Question: How can I use these pages to help me write a definition essay?

Teach/Model

Have students read the definition and bulleted points on p. 118. Mention that definition essays usually explain the meaning of abstract words or phrases as opposed to concrete objects that are easily defined. Have the students read the model.

Practice/Apply

Have students underline examples that support the definition throughout the essay.

Minilesson 106

Writing Opinions and Definitions

Common Core State Standard: W.6.2

Objective: State an opinion about the definition.

Guiding Question: How do I express my opinion about a definition?

Teach/Model

Tell students that the writer expresses an opinion about the word being defined at the beginning of the essay and provides details to support his opinion. Note that the writer also argues against views that are different from his opinion.

Practice/Apply

Have students underline the opinion of the writer, as well as opposing opinions. Discuss details that support the writer's opinion, and encourage students to suggest other opinions about technology.

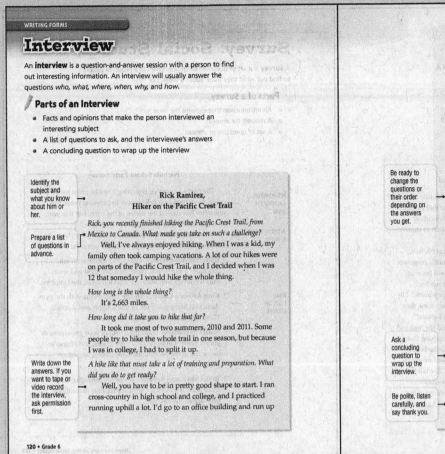

WRITING MODELS AND FORMS

Minilesson 107

Understanding the Interview

Common Core State Standard: W.6.9

Objective: Understand how to use the information presented about the interview.

Guiding Question: How can I use these pages to help me conduct an interview?

Teach/Model

Have students read the definition and bulleted points. Add that the person being interviewed is a source of information. Have students read the model. Point out that the writer thanks the subject at the end.

Practice/Apply

Have students underline the question words in each question (5Ws and H). Discuss the information given in the interviewee's answers.

Minilesson 108

Creating Good Interview Questions

Common Core State Standard: W.6.9

Objective: Use a variety of questions and be prepared to change them.

Guiding Question: How do I make sure I get the best information from my interview subject?

Teach/Model

Tell students that the writer asks a wide variety of questions. Note that the interviewer must be prepared to change questions or the order of questions, depending on how the interviewee answers, to get the most interesting information.

Practice/Apply

Have students review the interview and make up questions that they would ask the interviewee.

News Story/Survey

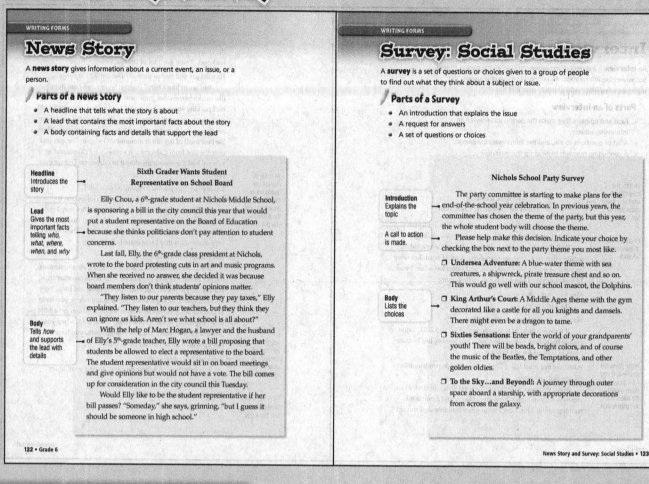

WRITING FORMS

News Story

A **news story** gives information about a current event, an issue, or a person.

Parts of a News Story

- A headline that tells what the story is about
- A lead that contains the most important facts about the story
- A body containing facts and details that support the lead

Headline
Introduces the story

Lead
Gives the most important facts telling *who, what, where, when,* and *why*

Body
Tells *how* and supports the lead with details

Sixth Grader Wants Student Representative on School Board

Elly Chou, a 6th-grade student at Nichols Middle School, is sponsoring a bill in the city council this year that would put a student representative on the Board of Education because she thinks politicians don't pay attention to student concerns.

Last fall, Elly, the 6th-grade class president at Nichols, wrote to the board protesting cuts in art and music programs. When she received no answer, she decided it was because board members don't think students' opinions matter.

"They listen to our parents because they pay taxes," Elly explained. "They listen to our teachers, but they think they can ignore us kids. Aren't we what school is all about?"

With the help of Marc Hogan, a lawyer and the husband of Elly's 5th-grade teacher, Elly wrote a bill proposing that students be allowed to elect a representative to the board. The student representative would sit in on board meetings and give opinions but would not have a vote. The bill comes up for consideration in the city council this Tuesday.

Would Elly like to be the student representative if her bill passes? "Someday," she says, grinning, "but I guess it should be someone in high school."

122 • Grade 6

WRITING FORMS

Survey: Social Studies

A **survey** is a set of questions or choices given to a group of people to find out what they think about a subject or issue.

Parts of a Survey

- An introduction that explains the issue
- A request for answers
- A set of questions or choices

Introduction
Explains the topic

A call to action is made.

Body
Lists the choices

Nichols School Party Survey

The party committee is starting to make plans for the end-of-the-school year celebration. In previous years, the committee has chosen the theme of the party, but this year, the whole student body will choose the theme.

Please help make this decision. Indicate your choice by checking the box next to the party theme you most like.

☐ **Undersea Adventure:** A blue-water theme with sea creatures, a shipwreck, pirate treasure chest and so on. This would go well with our school mascot, the Dolphins.

☐ **King Arthur's Court:** A Middle Ages theme with the gym decorated like a castle for all you knights and damsels. There might even be a dragon to tame.

☐ **Sixties Sensations:** Enter the world of your grandparents' youth! There will be beads, bright colors, and of course the music of the Beatles, the Temptations, and other golden oldies.

☐ **To the Sky...and Beyond!:** A journey through outer space aboard a starship, with appropriate decorations from across the galaxy.

News Story and Survey: Social Studies • 123

WRITING MODELS AND FORMS

Minilesson 109

Understanding the News Story

Common Core State Standard: W.6.4

Objective: Understand how to use the information presented about the news story.

Guiding Question: How can I use these pages to help me write a news story?

Teach/Model

Have students read the definition and bulleted points. Add that the writer answers the question *How* in the body of the news story. Have the students read the model.

Practice/Apply

Have students label each fact with the question it answers: *Who, What, Where, When, Why,* and *How.* Have them list other people they might interview if they wanted to expand the news story.

Minilesson 110

Understanding the Survey

Common Core State Standard: W.6.4

Objective: Understand how to use the information presented about the social studies survey.

Guiding Question: How can I use these pages to help me write and conduct a survey?

Teach/Model

Have students read the definition and bulleted points. Add that the writer includes a call to action at the beginning of the survey. Have the students read the model and discuss the choices.

Practice/Apply

Have students brainstorm a topic for a social studies survey, such as *field trip ideas* or *volunteer opportunities.* Together, write a survey that could be given to students at your school.

Business Letter/Science Observation Report

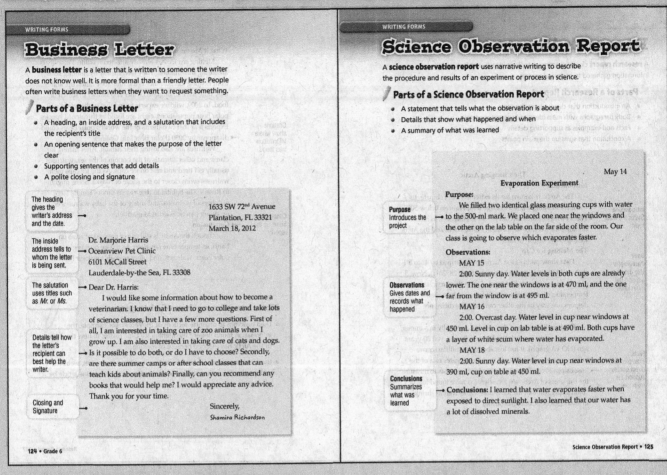

WRITING FORMS

Business Letter

A **business letter** is a letter that is written to someone the writer does not know well. It is more formal than a friendly letter. People often write business letters when they want to request something.

Parts of a Business Letter

- A heading, an inside address, and a salutation that includes the recipient's title
- An opening sentence that makes the purpose of the letter clear
- Supporting sentences that add details
- A polite closing and signature

The heading gives the writer's address and the date. →

1633 SW 72nd Avenue
Plantation, FL 33321
March 18, 2012

The inside address tells to whom the letter is being sent. →

Dr. Marjorie Harris
Oceanview Pet Clinic
6101 McCall Street
Lauderdale-by-the-Sea, FL 33308

The salutation uses titles such as *Mr.* or *Ms.* →

Dear Dr. Harris:

I would like some information about how to become a veterinarian. I know that I need to go to college and take lots of science classes, but I have a few more questions. First of all, I am interested in taking care of zoo animals when I grow up. I am also interested in taking care of cats and dogs.

Details tell how the letter's recipient can best help the writer. →

Is it possible to do both, or do I have to choose? Secondly, are there summer camps or after school classes that can teach kids about animals? Finally, can you recommend any books that would help me? I would appreciate any advice. Thank you for your time.

Closing and Signature

Sincerely,
Shamira Richardson

124 • Grade 6

WRITING FORMS

Science Observation Report

A **science observation report** uses narrative writing to describe the procedure and results of an experiment or process in science.

Parts of a Science Observation Report

- A statement that tells what the observation is about
- Details that show what happened and when
- A summary of what was learned

May 14

Evaporation Experiment

Purpose:

Purpose
Introduces the project

We filled two identical glass measuring cups with water to the 500-ml mark. We placed one near the windows and the other on the lab table on the far side of the room. Our class is going to observe which evaporates faster.

Observations:

Observations
Gives dates and records what happened

MAY 15

2:00. Sunny day. Water levels in both cups are already lower. The one near the windows is at 470 ml, and the one far from the window is at 495 ml.

MAY 16

2:00. Overcast day. Water level in cup near windows at 450 ml. Level in cup on lab table is at 490 ml. Both cups have a layer of white scum where water has evaporated.

MAY 18

2:00. Sunny day. Water level in cup near windows at 390 ml, cup on table at 450 ml.

Conclusions
Summarizes what was learned

Conclusions: I learned that water evaporates faster when exposed to direct sunlight. I also learned that our water has a lot of dissolved minerals.

Science Observation Report • 125

WRITING MODELS AND FORMS

Minilesson 111

Understanding the Business Letter

Common Core State Standard: W.6.4

Objective: Understand how to use the information presented about the business letter.

Guiding Question: How can I use these pages to help me write a business letter?

Teach/Model

Have students read p. 124. Remind them that business letters have a formal tone. Point out that the writer includes details that politely express what the writer needs the recipient to do.

Practice/Apply

Have students brainstorm to whom they might write a formal letter and why. Discuss why they should use a formal tone to write to this person.

Minilesson 112

Understanding the Science Observation Report

Common Core State Standard: W.6.10

Objective: Understand how to use the information presented about the science observation report.

Guiding Question: How can I use these pages to help me write a report on my scientific observations?

Teach/Model

Have students read the definition and bulleted points. Point out the chronological order of the recorded observations. Together, read the model. Add that the writer summarizes what was learned.

Practice/Apply

Have students organize the information in the observation report in a chart with headings.

Research Report

Research Report

A **research report** closely examines a topic or idea. It uses factual information gathered from several sources.

Parts of a Research Report

- An introduction that clearly states the topic
- Body paragraphs with main ideas and supporting details
- Facts and examples as supporting details
- A conclusion that sums up the main points

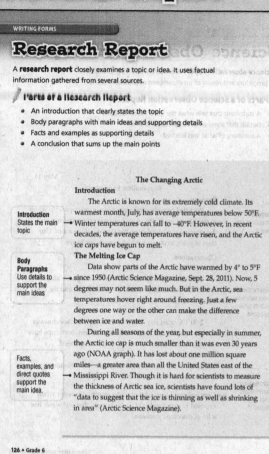

The Changing Arctic

Introduction

The Arctic is known for its extremely cold climate. Its warmest month, July, has average temperatures below 50°F. Winter temperatures can fall to –40°F. However, in recent decades, the average temperatures have risen, and the Arctic ice caps have begun to melt.

Introduction States the main topic

The Melting Ice Cap

Data show parts of the Arctic have warmed by 4° to 5°F since 1950 (Arctic Science Magazine, Sept. 28, 2011). Now, 5 degrees may not seem like much. But in the Arctic, sea temperatures hover right around freezing. Just a few degrees one way or the other can make the difference between ice and water.

Body Paragraphs Use details to support the main ideas

During all seasons of the year, but especially in summer, the Arctic ice cap is much smaller than it was even 30 years ago (NOAA graph). It has lost about one million square miles—a greater area than all the United States east of the Mississippi River. Though it is hard for scientists to measure the thickness of Arctic sea ice, scientists have found lots of "data to suggest that the ice is thinning as well as shrinking in area" (Arctic Science Magazine).

Facts, examples, and direct quotes support the main idea.

What it Means for Wildlife

Melting sea ice has already affected wildlife. Polar bears are losing their habitat. They feed mainly by hunting seals from floating ice. Summer is the time they fatten up, and they now have to migrate farther and farther in search of food. In 2009, wildlife experts found that of the world's 19 polar bear populations, eight are listed as threatened species. Experts fear that two-thirds of the world's polar bears could disappear by 2050 (Polar Bear Info Online).

Citations show where information was found.

Walruses are also losing their habitat. After fishing for clams and other animals at the bottom of the sea, walruses usually get tired and rest on ice caps. As the ice caps melt, walruses swim closer to the shore of Alaska. Some migrate to Russia. The habitat in those areas cannot handle large numbers of walruses, and many of the baby walruses end up dying (Arctic Science Magazine).

Conclusion Sums up the report

Conclusion

Though the Arctic is still one of the coldest areas on Earth, its temperature has risen. As the ice caps begin to melt, polar bears, walruses, and other animals lose their habitat.

Note how the author of this piece:

- Used headings to organize sections of the report. For example, the information found under "The Melting Ice Cap" relates to how the shape of the Arctic has changed because of melting.
- Used various sources for his information, including magazines, websites, and graphs. This writer also included the date of the magazine article he used.

WRITING MODELS AND FORMS

Minilesson 113

Understanding the Research Report

Common Core State Standard: W.6.7

Objective: Understand how to use the information presented about the research report.

Guiding Question: How can I use these pages to help me write a good research report?

Teach/Model

Have students read the definition and bulleted points. Tell students that a research report should cover a topic that is clearly defined in the introduction and summed up in the conclusion.

Practice/Apply

Have students read the model. Go over the parts of the report with students. Ask students to rewrite the conclusion in their own words.

Minilesson 114

Citing Sources in a Research Report

Common Core State Standard: W.6.8

Objective: Write citations for sources used in a report.

Guiding Question: How do I write citations for my sources?

Teach/Model

Explain to students that each source used to write a research report will need a citation either in the report itself or on a separate Works Cited page. Point out to students how the writer of the model cited his sources in the report.

Practice/Apply

Have students find another source that contains information about the Arctic ice caps. Have them write a sentence with a citation that could be added to the model.

Graphs, Diagrams, and Charts

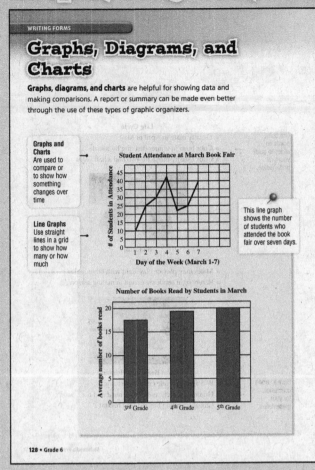

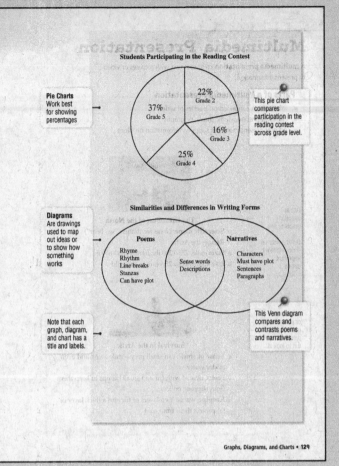

Minilesson 115

Understanding Graphs, Diagrams, and Charts

Common Core State Standard: W.6.2a

Objective: Understand how to use the information presented about graphs, diagrams, and charts.

Guiding Question: How can I use these pages to help me create good graphics for my reports?

Teach/Model

Have students read the top of p. 128. Explain to students that the type of information they need to present will determine the type of graphic they use.

Practice/Apply

Review the models. Discuss the type of information presented in each. Ask students to compare the different types of graphs, diagrams, and charts and suggest possible uses for each.

Minilesson 116

Making a Chart

Common Core State Standard: W.6.2a

Objective: Use a chart in a research report.

Guiding Question: How do I use a chart in a research report?

Teach/Model

Review some possible ways to display data, such as a bar graph, a pie chart, or a Venn diagram. Point to the pie chart on p. 129. Explain that a chart like this can help illustrate data in a clear way.

Practice/Apply

Take a quick survey of the class. Ask students to give their favorite color. Write the data on the board. Ask students to determine which kind of chart or graph is best for displaying this information. Work with students to draw the appropriate chart.

Writing for Common Core • **101**

Multimedia Presentation

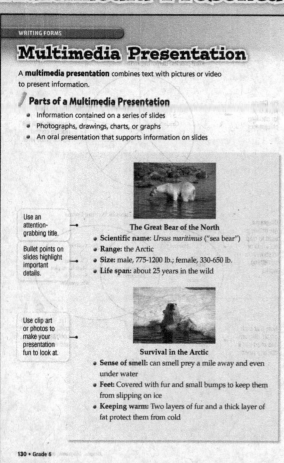

WRITING FORMS

Multimedia Presentation

A **multimedia presentation** combines text with pictures or video to present information.

Parts of a Multimedia Presentation
- Information contained on a series of slides
- Photographs, drawings, charts, or graphs
- An oral presentation that supports information on slides

Use an attention-grabbing title.

Bullet points on slides highlight important details.

Use clip art or photos to make your presentation fun to look at.

The Great Bear of the North
- **Scientific name:** *Ursus maritimus* ("sea bear")
- **Range:** the Arctic
- **Size:** male, 775-1200 lb.; female, 330-650 lb.
- **Life span:** about 25 years in the wild

Survival in the Arctic
- **Sense of smell:** can smell prey a mile away and even under water
- **Feet:** Covered with fur and small bumps to keep them from slipping on ice
- **Keeping warm:** Two layers of fur and a thick layer of fat protect them from cold

130 • Grade 6

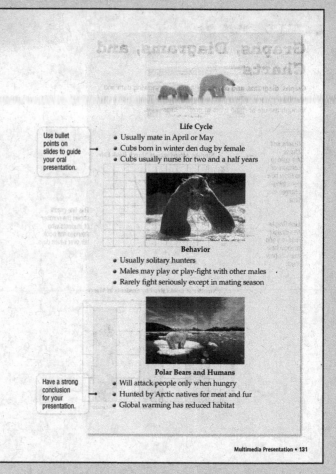

Use bullet points on slides to guide your oral presentation.

Life Cycle
- Usually mate in April or May
- Cubs born in winter den dug by female
- Cubs usually nurse for two and a half years

Behavior
- Usually solitary hunters
- Males may play or play-fight with other males
- Rarely fight seriously except in mating season

Have a strong conclusion for your presentation.

Polar Bears and Humans
- Will attack people only when hungry
- Hunted by Arctic natives for meat and fur
- Global warming has reduced habitat

Multimedia Presentation • 131

WRITING MODELS AND FORMS

Minilesson 117

Understanding the Multimedia Presentation

Common Core State Standard: W.6.6

Objective: Understand how to use the information presented about multimedia presentations.

Guiding Question: How can I use these pages to help me create good multimedia presentations?

Teach/Model

Have students read the definition and bulleted points. Explain to students that a multimedia presentation can be used for almost any type of report.

Practice/Apply

Go over the model on pp. 130–131. Model an oral presentation to accompany the first slide. Ask for volunteers to repeat this activity with the other slides.

Minilesson 118

Creating Attention-Grabbing Titles and Headings

Common Core State Standard: W.6.6

Objective: Write attention-grabbing titles and headings.

Guiding Question: How do I write attention-grabbing titles and headings for a multimedia presentation?

Teach/Model

With students, read the title and headings in the model. Point out that the title and headings accurately describe what information will be presented.

Practice/Apply

Give students a topic, such as rainforest animals. Have students write a title and four headings for a multimedia presentation about the topic.

Personal Narrative

Personal Narrative

A **personal narrative** tells a true story about an experience in the writer's life, how it made the writer feel, and why it was important.

Parts of a Personal Narrative

- An opening sentence, or lead, that gets the reader's attention
- Several sentences that introduce the topic of the story
- A body that shows events in chronological order, or sequence
- Details and dialogue
- An ending that tells how the story worked out or what the writer learned

Pilgrim for a Day

Beginning
Attention-getting first sentence

I celebrated Thanksgiving last year with the Pilgrims and the Native Americans. Well, actually it was the day after Thanksgiving, and the Pilgrims were really actors in costumes. We were spending the holiday weekend with my aunt and uncle in Boston, and as a special treat they took us out for a day at Plimoth Plantation. It's a big outdoor history museum in Plymouth, Massachusetts, a short way from where the real Pilgrims had their colonial village.

Sentences that clearly show what the story is about

We left the 21ˢᵗ century behind minutes after Aunt Lynn parked the van. First we walked through a gate in a tall wooden fence called a palisade. Next we followed a path with cows grazing on each side. This brought us into a village of homes, barns, and shops with thatched roofs. Men and women wearing seventeenth-century clothes were going about their business as if it were 1627.

Middle
Describes events in time order

We spent a while just looking around and poking into the houses and stores. Then I overcame my shyness and talked to people.

Vivid details about what the narrator saw and heard

Other Transitions
Minutes after
First
Next
A while
Then
After lunch
Last

Narrator's personal thoughts, feelings, and opinions

They sound more English than American, and they talk the way English was spoken in the 1600s, but it wasn't hard to understand them. Each actor takes the role of an actual person of the Plymouth colony. We talked with a blacksmith, a farm wife taking goods to market, and a leather worker.

A woman cooking soup in a kettle over a fireplace was the most interesting. She talked about the ingredients in her soup, how she grew them, and how she stored them so that they wouldn't spoil. Her voice turned grim when I asked her about the voyage from England. She described how many people had died, including her own baby. Her story was so sad that I had to remind myself that she was only playing a role, like in a movie!

After lunch, we wandered down the hill to the Wampanoag village. Those were the Indians from the Thanksgiving story. The people in this village are not role players. They are actual Native Americans, though not all are Wampanoags. They talk about their customs and show how their ancestors made things like arrows and canoes.

The last thing we visited was in the town of Plymouth itself. It has the *Mayflower II*, a copy of the ship that brought the real Plymouth colonists to America. The sailors were role-players too. They talked about how they sailed the ship and how they make things like rope and sails.

Ending
Tells what the writer learned

By then we were all tired and ready for some turkey leftovers. But I probably won't think the same way about Thanksgiving ever again. For one thing, the actors at Plimoth Plantation looked puzzled when I asked about "the first Thanksgiving" that they celebrated with the Native Americans. After a while they pretended to figure out that I meant the "harvest festival" they celebrated in 1621. As for the "Pilgrims," they had no idea what I was talking about when I called them that. It turns out that people didn't call the Plymouth colonists by that name until 200 years later!

WRITING MODELS AND FORMS

Minilesson 119

Understanding the Personal Narrative

Common Core State Standard: W.6.3

Objective: Understand how to use the information presented about the personal narrative.

Guiding Question: How can I use these pages to help me write a good personal narrative?

Teach/Model

Have students read the definition and bulleted points on p. 132. Add that a personal narrative is always written in the first person.

Practice/Apply

Have students read the model. Go over the parts of the personal narrative illustrated by the boxes. Have students identify the places where the writer expresses thoughts and feelings about the experience.

Minilesson 120

Writing a Strong Beginning

Common Core State Standard: W.6.3a

Objective: Write a strong beginning.

Guiding Question: How do I write a strong beginning for my personal narrative?

Teach/Model

Reread the first paragraph of the model with students. Point out that the first sentence grabs the readers' attention while the rest of the paragraph introduces the setting and main characters.

Practice/Apply

Have students write the first paragraph for a personal narrative about the first day of school. Have pairs compare their opening sentences and suggest ways to make them more interesting.

Biography

Biography

A **biography** is a true story of a person's life and achievements.

Parts of a Biography

- Reasons why the subject is worthy of a biography
- Key dates and events in the person's life
- Explanation of how these events affected the subject

Stephen Hawking

Beginning Identifies the subject and a key event or fact about his life

When Stephen Hawking was 21, he was stricken with a terrible nerve sickness called ALS. It is also known as Lou Gehrig's disease, after a famous baseball player who died from it. Nearly everyone who gets ALS dies within two years, but Hawking has lived with it for 49 years. In fact, he has lived to become one of the most famous scientists in the world.

This paragraph gives information about his birth and early life.

Stephen Hawking was born in Oxford, England, on January 8, 1942. His father was a doctor who studied tropical diseases. He urged his bright son to seek a career in science. Stephen decided that medicine and biology weren't exact enough for him, so he turned to math and physics. He entered Oxford University at age 17 and graduated with honors three years later. His goal as a scientist was to study nothing less than the structure of the whole universe! But then he learned that he had ALS. It eventually led to his being confined to a wheelchair and losing the ability to speak.

Middle Describes personal details and events in the person's life

One of his professors urged Stephen to continue his studies despite his disability. In 1965, Hawking married Jane Wilde. His marriage gave him the courage to pursue his career in science. A year later, he became a

Sequence Clues
January 8, 1942
Age 17
Three years later
1965
A year later
During the 1970s and 1980s
1988

professor at Cambridge University in England. He has been a teacher and researcher there ever since. He and his wife eventually had three children.

Hawking's main work has been with black holes. These are the mysterious objects in space that are so dense that nothing can escape them, not even light, because their gravity is too strong. Hawking proved that the universe could have started as something like a black hole—a single point that contained all the matter in the universe. This work showed how the "Big Bang" theory of how the universe began could be true. He demonstrated that the universe is filled with mini black holes, left over from that Big Bang.

These paragraphs show what the subject did that made him famous.

Hawking's work won him many scientific awards during the 1970s and 1980s. Most of his work can be understood only by other scientists. But in 1988, he published *A Brief History of Time: From the Big Bang to Black Holes*. This book explained his ideas to ordinary readers. It became a best seller and made him a public celebrity.

Hawking can speak only with the aid of an electronic device. But that hasn't kept him from making many TV appearances. Besides several interviews, he has appeared on shows like *Star Trek* and *The Simpsons*. He also speaks frequently to wheelchair-bound young people.

Ending Summarizes the subject's life and achievements

Stephen Hawking is still trying to understand how all the known forces of the universe fit together. This was a problem that even the great Albert Einstein couldn't solve. As Hawking has said, "My goal is a complete understanding of the universe, why it is as it is, and why it exists at all."

134 • Grade 6

Biography • 135

WRITING MODELS AND FORMS

Minilesson 121

Understanding the Biography

Common Core State Standard: W.6.8

Objective: Understand how to use the information presented about the biography.

Guiding Question: How can I use these pages to help me write a good biography?

Teach/Model

Have students read the definition and bulleted points. Explain that a biography covers the most important parts of a person's life to date.

Practice/Apply

Have students read the model. Go over the callout boxes labeling parts of the biography. Ask why the subject is worthy of a biography. Next, ask students to list the important events in the subject's life.

Minilesson 122

Using Time-Order Transitions

Common Core State Standard: W.6.3c

Objective: Use transitional words and phrases to show a time relationship between events.

Guiding Question: How do I use transitional words and phrases to show a time relationship between events?

Teach/Model

Reread the model with students. Point out to students the transitions used by the writer to indicate the time relationship between events in the text.

Practice/Apply

Write a list of time-order transitions on the board. Have students go through the model and suggest alternatives for the transitions used by the author.

Fictional Narrative

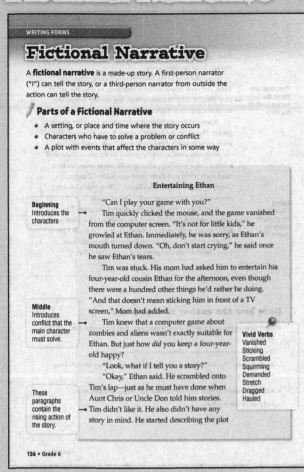

Fictional Narrative

A **fictional narrative** is a made-up story. A first-person narrator ("I") can tell the story, or a third-person narrator from outside the action can tell the story.

Parts of a Fictional Narrative

- A setting, or place and time where the story occurs
- Characters who have to solve a problem or conflict
- A plot with events that affect the characters in some way

Entertaining Ethan

Beginning Introduces the characters →

"Can I play your game with you?"

Tim quickly clicked the mouse, and the game vanished from the computer screen. "It's not for little kids," he growled at Ethan. Immediately, he was sorry, as Ethan's mouth turned down. "Oh, don't start crying," he said once he saw Ethan's tears.

Tim was stuck. His mom had asked him to entertain his four-year-old cousin Ethan for the afternoon, even though there were a hundred other things he'd rather be doing. "And that doesn't mean sticking him in front of a TV screen," Mom had added.

Middle Introduces conflict that the main character must solve. →

Tim knew that a computer game about zombies and aliens wasn't exactly suitable for Ethan. But just how *did* you keep a four-year-old happy?

"Look, what if I tell you a story?"

"Okay," Ethan said. He scrambled onto Tim's lap—just as he must have done when Aunt Chris or Uncle Don told him stories.

These paragraphs contain the rising action of the story. →

Tim didn't like it. He also didn't have any story in mind. He started describing the plot

Vivid Verbs
Vanished
Sticking
Scrambled
Squirming
Demanded
Stretch
Dragged
Hauled

Dialogue lets readers imagine what characters sound like and what each character is feeling.

of one of his favorite movies. But Ethan got bored and started squirming. He dropped the story and started another, but Ethan didn't understand it any better than he had understood the first.

"Tell me a story about a giant bird," Ethan demanded.

"I don't *know* any stories about birds!" Tim said. It was only two o'clock, and the afternoon seemed to stretch ahead like a jail sentence.

Then Tim remembered his little-kid toys. He'd wanted to sell them at a sidewalk sale, but Mom had stuck them away in a closet. "Look, how about we build something?" he said.

"Okay," Ethan said, scrambling off Tim's lap.

Tim dragged a cardboard box out of the closet. It was full of wooden pieces with holes in them and wooden fasteners for putting them together. He saw Ethan's eyes get big. "Let's build a power machine!" Ethan said.

This paragraph shows the climax, or the high point of the story.

"Sure," Tim said, and he thought that maybe now he could get back to his computer game.

Then he saw that Ethan was having trouble fitting the pieces together. "Here, let me help you," he said.

"Okay, but I'm the captain!" Ethan said. "You can help, but I get to say how we build the machine."

"Sure," Tim said. He hauled out another box, this one filled with plastic blocks.

"Man, we can build a whole *city!*" Ethan exclaimed.

"Well, let's start with the power machine," Tim said, remembering how much fun he'd had with those toys. "Go on, captain, tell me what we should do."

They were still building when Uncle Don came to pick up Ethan.

Ending Shows how the characters solved the conflict. →

"Just give us five more minutes," Ethan begged.

Uncle Don looked at Tim. "Is that okay with you?"

Tim grinned. "You heard the captain. Five more minutes."

136 • Grade 6

Fictional Narrative • 137

Minilesson 123

Understanding the Fictional Narrative

Common Core State Standard: W.6.3

Objective: Understand how to use the information presented about the fictional narrative.

Guiding Question: How can I use these pages to help me write a good fictional narrative?

Teach/Model

Have students read the definition and bulleted points. Add that the ending of a fictional narrative follows the resolution of the conflict.

Practice/Apply

Have students read the model. Have them identify and list the main characters, setting, major plot points, and conflict. Discuss with students how the conflict was resolved.

Minilesson 124

Writing Dialogue

Common Core State Standard: W.6.3

Objective: Use realistic dialogue in a fictional narrative.

Guiding Question: How do I use realistic dialogue in a fictional narrative?

Teach/Model

Reread the model with students. Have students read the dialogue in the story aloud. Point out that the dialogue sounds realistic and tells the reader about the characters while moving the plot along.

Practice/Apply

Have students work in pairs to write dialogue for a fictional narrative about two students who have to solve a problem together. Ask for volunteers to share their work with the class.

Fantasy Story

Fantasy Story

A **fantasy story** uses magic or other unreal ideas as a main part of the plot, characters, or setting.

Parts of a Fantasy Story

- Characters who have to solve a problem or conflict
- Made up elements that are not like real life
- Themes from traditional myths, legends, or folklore

The Third Test

Beginning
Introduces the conflict

The forest was a maze. The paths seemed to wind and branch off forever without an exit. Several times Trina thought she had found her way out, only to reach another dead end. She heard the roar of a dragon and the groans of things even worse. She might die here. Then her father would remain in the dungeon of the witch-queen Zulora.

A flashback can tell about earlier events.

Trina felt hopeless. She could imagine Zulora laughing in her tower. Trina had struggled to pass the queen's first two tests. She had climbed Mount Evyll, guarded by crazy monkeys with sharp teeth, to bring back the rare and glittering Amethyst Flower jewel. She had traveled deep into the dark and scary cave of Lothar the Dwarf. She had charmed Lothar into giving her the strange jewel that he said would help her pass this third test and defeat the queen. The jewel lay heavy in her pocket, but so far it was useless.

Middle
Shows how character faces problem

Now the path was getting wider. That might mean Trina was near the exit! *Keep turning right,* she thought.

A hiss interrupted her thoughts. Two threatening eyes glowed in the darkness.

Descriptive Adjectives
Hideous
Glittering
Bleak
Fearsome
Inert
Baleful
Trembling

This paragraph shows the turning point of the story.

They belonged to a giant cat with horns, and she was the mouse. Trina sprinted away.

Now she was as far away as ever from getting out. Tired, she sank down on the forest floor. At least the bed of pine needles made it comfortable. She needed to rest. She lay down and closed her eyes. Just a quick nap, and then...

A sound like crystal bells was coming from her apron pocket. She drew out Lothar's jewel. It was glowing! The jewel grew larger in her hands until it was a slab of glass.

Moments later, a map appeared on the glass. It showed a forest and a winding pathway with many branches and dead ends. Here and there were words like "Danger: Dragon," and "Danger: Quicksand." There was a blinking arrow next to words that said, "This way out!"

Ending
Shows how the character solved the conflict

A light was blinking in the center of the glass. Trina wasted no time. She followed the arrow and the blinking light moved with her until she was out of the maze. Queen Zulora's castle lay just ahead, and with the magic map, Trina could defeat the queen and rescue her father.

Note how the author of this piece:

- Used sensory details to make vivid descriptions that the reader can imagine.

  She heard the roar of a dragon and the groans of things even worse.

  She had climbed Mount Evyll, guarded by crazy monkeys with sharp teeth, to bring back the rare and glittering Amethyst Flower jewel.

- Allowed readers to hear the main character's important thoughts.

  Just a quick nap, and then...

138 • Grade 6

Fantasy Story • 139

Minilesson 125

Understanding the Fantasy Story

Common Core State Standard: W.6.3

Objective: Understand how to use the information presented about the fantasy story.

Guiding Question: How can I use these pages to help me write a good fantasy story?

Teach/Model

Have students read the definition and bulleted points. Explain that a fantasy story is a fictional narrative that contains elements of magic or make-believe.

Practice/Apply

Have students read the model. Go over the parts of the story labeled by callout boxes. Ask students to identify the elements of the story that indicate it is a fantasy story.

106 • Writing for Common Core

Minilesson 126

Using Sensory Details

Common Core State Standard: W.6.3d

Objective: Use sensory details to create vivid descriptions.

Guiding Question: How do I use sensory details to create vivid descriptions?

Teach/Model

Reread the model with students. Have students identify sensory words used by the author, such as *threatening eyes glowed in the darkness* and *a sound like crystal bells.*

Practice/Apply

Have students work in pairs to rewrite the second paragraph of the model using different sensory words to create new descriptions. Tell them to keep the tone and general meaning of the sentences. Have students share their work with the class.

Play

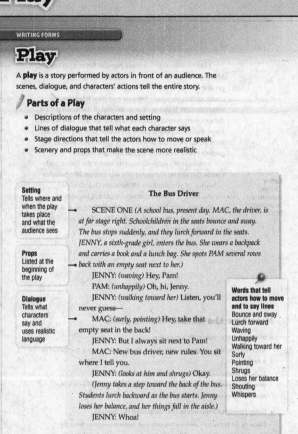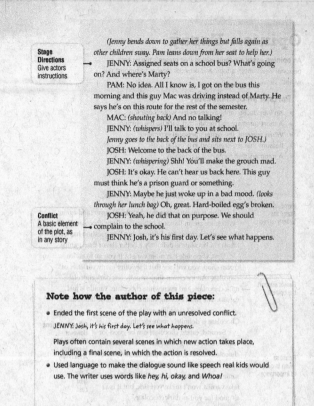

WRITING MODELS AND FORMS

Minilesson 127

Understanding the Play

Common Core State Standard: W.6.3b

Objective: Understand how to use the information presented about the play.
Guiding Question: How can I use these pages to help me write a good play?

Teach/Model

Have students read the definition and bulleted points on p. 140. Tell students that they should be able to visualize what a play looks like on stage as they read.

Practice/Apply

Have students read the play aloud. Go over the parts of the play labeled in the boxes. Ask students to identify the main conflict and discuss how the stage directions help to bring the play to life.

Minilesson 128

Writing a Play

Common Core State Standard: W.6.3b

Objective: Write dialogue for a play.
Guiding Question: How do I write dialogue for a play?

Teach/Model

Have students reread the model. Point out that the writer used realistic dialogue to move the plot forward. Remind students that using informal word choice helps to create dialogue that sounds like real sixth-graders talking.

Practice/Apply

Have students work in small groups to write the next scene in the play. Remind students to use stage directions and read the dialogue aloud to make sure it sounds realistic. Have volunteers read their scenes to the class.

Opinion Essay

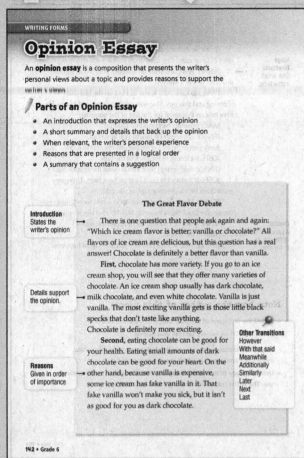

Opinion Essay

An **opinion essay** is a composition that presents the writer's personal views about a topic and provides reasons to support the writer's views.

Parts of an Opinion Essay

- An introduction that expresses the writer's opinion
- A short summary and details that back up the opinion
- When relevant, the writer's personal experience
- Reasons that are presented in a logical order
- A summary that contains a suggestion

Introduction
States the writer's opinion

Details support the opinion.

Reasons
Given in order of importance

The Great Flavor Debate

There is one question that people ask again and again: "Which ice cream flavor is better: vanilla or chocolate?" All flavors of ice cream are delicious, but this question has a real answer! Chocolate is definitely a better flavor than vanilla.

First, chocolate has more variety. If you go to an ice cream shop, you will see that they offer many varieties of chocolate. An ice cream shop usually has dark chocolate, milk chocolate, and even white chocolate. Vanilla is just vanilla. The most exciting vanilla gets is those little black specks that don't taste like anything. Chocolate is definitely more exciting.

Second, eating chocolate can be good for your health. Eating small amounts of dark chocolate can be good for your heart. On the other hand, because vanilla is expensive, some ice cream has fake vanilla in it. That fake vanilla won't make you sick, but it isn't as good for you as dark chocolate.

Other Transitions
However
With that said
Meanwhile
Additionally
Similarly
Later
Next
Last

Finally, chocolate is a more popular flavor than vanilla. My school has an ice cream station, and we are allowed to get one ice cream treat on Fridays. I have to get to the ice cream station very early because everyone takes the chocolate first. If you wait until the end of the lunch period, the ice cream station will have only vanilla left. This is how I know that most people prefer chocolate. If most people like something, that thing must be very good! Plus, both of my parents prefer chocolate, and so does my brother.

Ice cream is a fantastic treat no matter the flavor, and vanilla can still be exciting if you mix in fruit, like bananas or berries. If you must decide between chocolate and vanilla, though, always choose chocolate. Chocolate is healthier for your heart and has more variety, so it is more exciting. Plus, most people prefer chocolate, so you'll get to share the experience with your friends.

Ending
Contains summary and recommendation

Note how the author of this piece:

- Introduced the essay with a question.
  Another way she could have introduced the essay is to use a quotation or a fact.
  Jo Brand wisely said, "Anything is good if it's made of chocolate." .
  When I surveyed my homeroom class, I found out that 24 out of 30 people like chocolate ice cream better than vanilla.
- Shared personal experiences that supported her opinion.
  I have to get to the ice cream station very early because everyone takes the chocolate first …This is how I know that most people prefer chocolate.

142 • Grade 6

Opinion Essay • 143

WRITING MODELS AND FORMS

Minilesson 129

Introducing the Opinion Essay

Common Core State Standards: W.6.1a, W.6.1e

Objective: Understand how to use the handbook pages to write an effective opinion essay.

Guiding Question: How do I write about my opinion?

Teach/Model

Have students read pp. 142–143. Point out that the boldfaced transitions highlight each reason. Add that the writer's opinion is stated strongly. She did not say, "I think…" Instead, she stated, "Chocolate is definitely a better flavor…" Her strong language helps to convince readers.

Practice/Apply

Have students identify the writer's reasons for her opinion. Discuss how transition words help to organize the ideas.

Minilesson 130

Supporting an Opinion

Common Core State Standard: W.6.1b

Objective: Include evidence to support opinions.

Guiding Question: How do I explain the reasons why my opinion is valid?

Teach/Model

Point out that the student writer included three reasons to support her opinion and that each of these reasons is the topic sentence of a separate paragraph. Rather than simply stating the reasons, she included an entire paragraph of details to explain each.

Practice/Apply

Have students write a topic sentence about their favorite flavor of ice cream. Then have them add sentences with details and examples to support their opinion.

Persuasive Essay

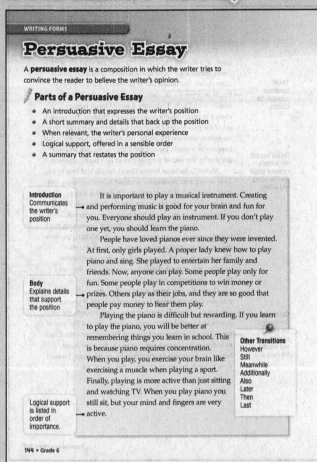

Persuasive Essay

A **persuasive essay** is a composition in which the writer tries to convince the reader to believe the writer's opinion.

Parts of a Persuasive Essay

- An introduction that expresses the writer's position
- A short summary and details that back up the position
- When relevant, the writer's personal experience
- Logical support, offered in a sensible order
- A summary that restates the position

Introduction
Communicates the writer's position

It is important to play a musical instrument. Creating and performing music is good for your brain and fun for you. Everyone should play an instrument. If you don't play one yet, you should learn the piano.

Body
Explains details that support the position

People have loved pianos ever since they were invented. At first, only girls played. A proper lady knew how to play piano and sing. She played to entertain her family and friends. Now, anyone can play. Some people play only for fun. Some people play in competitions to win money or prizes. Others play as their jobs, and they are so good that people pay money to hear them play.

Playing the piano is difficult but rewarding. If you learn to play the piano, you will be better at remembering things you learn in school. This is because piano requires concentration. When you play, you exercise your brain like exercising a muscle when playing a sport. Finally, playing is more active than just sitting and watching TV. When you play piano you still sit, but your mind and fingers are very active.

Logical support is listed in order of importance.

Other Transitions
However
Still
Meanwhile
Additionally
Also
Later
Then
Last

144 • Grade 6

To play the piano, you sit on a wooden bench and put your hands on the 88 black and white keys. It is very hard to play because you don't just make up what notes to hit. You have to read music. Music looks like a lot of black dots on a piece of paper. Learning to read music is like learning another language. If you know how to read music, you can talk to the piano. You can make it sing! You can also write your own music. Then, strangers can play the song you invented!

I have played the piano since I was 5 years old. Piano is very fun for me because when I play it, *I* am the one making music. I sit, I move my fingers, and I get to hear a beautiful song. I play songs written by famous people from the past, such as Beethoven and Debussy. I also play songs from my favorite movies and TV shows. I like playing piano because it makes me feel creative.

Playing piano is one of many options in music, and in my opinion, it is the best. Playing piano is great because it is a healthy, fun hobby. You'll love making beautiful music. Once you start playing piano, you won't want to stop!

Ending
Summarizes the main arguments

Note how the author of this piece:

- Shared a relevant personal experience.
  I have played the piano since I was 5 years old.
- Concluded the essay by summarizing her main arguments. Another way to end a persuasive essay is to include a fact or a description.
  Only 1% of adults play an instrument. If everyone learns to play piano, we can make the world a more musical place.
  Imagine sitting at a piano and putting your hands on the cool, glossy keys. You press down and hear your own sweet melody.

Persuasive Essay • 145

WRITING MODELS AND FORMS

Minilesson 131

Introducing the Persuasive Essay

Common Core State Standards: W.6.1a, W.6.1e

Objective: Understand the characteristics of a strong persuasive essay.

Guiding Question: How can I convince readers to agree with my ideas?

Teach/Model

Have students read pp. 144–145. Point out that the introduction includes the word *should*, and explain that persuasive essays often include convincing words such as *should, need to,* and *best.*

Practice/Apply

Point out that the details are listed in order of importance. Have students discuss what makes some details more important than others.

Minilesson 132

Writing a Strong Conclusion

Common Core State Standard: W.6.1e

Objective: Provide a conclusion for a persuasive essay.

Guiding Question: How should I end my persuasive essay?

Teach/Model

Reread the opinion statement in the introduction and then the final paragraph. Point out that the conclusion restates the opinion and summarizes the main arguments. Explain that this reminds readers of the writer's opinion and the most important ideas. Point out that the student writer spoke directly to readers and related how playing piano would benefit them.

Practice/Apply

Have small groups work together to write a new conclusion for the essay.

Response to a Play

WRITING FORMS

Response to a Play

A **response to a play** is an essay that analyzes the script of a play and states the writer's opinion of it.

Parts of a Response to a Play

- The writer's opinion of the play
- An analysis of the play's characters, plot, and setting
- An opinion of how the text will work as a dramatic performance
- Details from the text that support the writer's opinion

The Junkman's Star Cruise by Frank Maltesi

Introduction
States the writer's main idea in a topic sentence

A science-fiction movie with special effects can make you believe that you're on an alien planet or a future Earth. Can a play, presented live on a stage, bring settings like these to life too? That's the question I asked when I read Frank Maltesi's sci-fi play, *The Junkman's Star Cruise*.

The "junkman" is David Wax, a man who works on a space station in the year 2190. Maltesi's stage directions describe the setting as a plain working world. Scenes take place in labs, offices, and a cafeteria. The only setting that seems out-of-this-world is a small shuttle-like spaceship.

Body
Describes the setting, plot, and main characters

David's boss at the space station is afraid that aliens from another planet will start a war with Earth. David would almost welcome something exciting like that. His two astronaut friends, Janice and Pete, get to explore new planets, but David finds his job boring. He calls himself the junkman because his job is to control a computer that shoots laser beams at garbage that floats through space. He zaps broken satellites and other electronics so that they won't be a danger to space flight. David feels that nothing interesting will ever happen to him.

146 • Grade 6

These opinions establish the conflict.

Then David's computer sees a space probe heading for Earth on a strange flight path. His boss, the strict Dr. Shirley Freed, thinks it's a secret space weapon from a dangerous alien planet. She orders David to destroy the space probe, but he believes it's an alien probe sent to make friendly contact with Earth. To destroy it would mean ruining a chance to learn about a non-human civilization. The second act of the play shows David and his astronaut friends' secret mission to examine the probe, what they discover, and what happens as a result. I won't spoil the ending, but let's just say that by the end of the play David isn't bored anymore.

Details support the author's opinions about the characters and setting.

Maltesi's dialogue brings David, Janice, and Pete to life. They reveal their reasons for wanting to work in space and their common love for adventure. Dr. Freed is a less successful character. She seems like the tough police chief or tough boss from any book, television show, or movie.

The plot and characters make the play interesting, but I have to wonder how it plays on the stage. Maltesi describes the settings in general terms, such as the space station "looking unfinished, like a building under construction" and the view of Earth through a window. Only the probe itself is described in detailed stage directions.

Conclusion
Summarizes the writer's point of view and restates the main idea

One of the fun things about reading science fiction is that you can imagination the strange settings. If you are watching a science-fiction movie or a play, though, the set design and special effects need to make you feel like you're there. I would recommend reading *The Junkman's Star Cruise* to anyone who likes science fiction. On the other hand, before I'd recommend seeing the play on the stage, I would have to see if the sets really bring the play to life.

Response to a Play • 147

WRITING MODELS AND FORMS

Minilesson 133

Introducing the Response to a Play

Common Core State Standards: W.6.1a, W.6.1e

Objective: Use the pages to understand how to write a response to a play.

Guiding Question: What should I include when writing about a play?

Teach/Model

Have students read pp. 146–147. Explain that the main idea is often a statement; then point out that it is written as a question and answer in this example. Add that writers can include both positive and negative opinions of the play.

Practice/Apply

Have students underline the writer's opinions in the model. Discuss whether they are properly supported.

Minilesson 134

Using Details from the Text

Common Core State Standard: W.6.1b

Objective: Use evidence from the text to support the main idea.

Guiding Question: How can I use examples from the play to explain my opinions about it?

Teach/Model

Explain that evidence from the play is included to support the main idea of the response. Point out that some of the details are restated in the student's own words, and other details are quoted from the play. Remind students that exact words from the text must be written in quotation marks.

Practice/Apply

Have students identify details from the play that were restated by the student writer. Then, have them locate the details that were quoted from the text.

Author Response

Author Response

An **author response** is an essay about the works of a specific writer. It is not a response to a single book but a report on an author's style as shown by two or more works.

Parts of an Author Response

- Facts about the author and his or her books
- The writer's opinion or point of view about the author

Andrew Clements, Author of Realistic Fantasy

Introduction
Gives the main idea of the essay

Andrew Clements must be young at heart. If not, he has an incredible memory of what it's like to be a kid in school. Most of his books are about school and what goes on between kids and their classmates and teachers. That part of Clements's books is always so realistic that you might not realize that he is often writing fantasy.

Body
Contains details that support the main idea

Take for instance Clements's book *Frindle*, which I read in the fourth grade. The main character of *Frindle*, Nick Allen, is fascinated by words. One day he asks his teacher, Mrs. Granger, where words come from. He wants to know who decides that the animal that barks and wags its tail should be called a dog. The teacher replies, "You do,"

This paragraph explains how the writer's view of the author applies to one book.

meaning that a word means whatever the people who speak a language say it means. This gives Nick the idea that if he starts calling a pen a "frindle," maybe he can start a movement to change the word—and he does. By the time Nick's parents and Mrs. Granger get annoyed enough to try to stop it, a pen is called a frindle all over town. When you think about it, you know something like that could never happen. It's no more real than the wizards in *Harry Potter*. But because school is presented in such a realistic way, you can almost believe it. And that's why *Frindle* is fun.

These paragraphs compare two of the author's books, showing how they both illustrate the writer's main idea.

I didn't realize this about *Frindle* until I read Clements's *School Story* this year. Natalie Nelson is a 6th-grade girl who is a really good writer. She lives in New York, where her mother is a children's book editor at a publishing company. Natalie writes a story that is so good that her friend Zoe Reisman talks her into sending it to her mom's company under a fake name. So far *School Story* is completely realistic, even though it's a stretch that a 6th grader could write a book that's good enough to be published. But then *School Story* takes a wacky turn. Zoe poses as an author's agent to try to sell Natalie's book—and gets away with it. When they need an adult to keep the deception going, Zoe talks their teacher, Ms. Clayton, into joining them—and she agrees!

Here, as in *Frindle*, Andrew Clements is stretching the definition of "realistic fiction." When you take a step back and think about what's going on, you *know* that a 12-year-old like Zoe could never get away with impersonating an adult, even by e-mail. Also, can you imagine a teacher behaving like Ms. Clayton and not getting fired? The book is so well set in the world we all know, the world of homework, 6th-grade social life, and busy parents, that the story feels true.

Conclusion
Gives a summary of the main idea

The schools in Andrew Clements's stories are always real places, even when the situations may be a little fantastic—or a lot, like the boy who turns invisible in *Things Not Seen*. His readers may be too young to know much about the world, but we do know school! And so does Andrew Clements.

WRITING MODELS AND FORMS

Minilesson 135

Introducing the Author Response

Common Core State Standards: W.6.1.a, W.6.1.b

Objective: Recognize the qualities of a strong author response.

Guiding Question: How do I share my ideas about an author?

Teach/Model

Have students read pp. 148 and 149. Add that although an author response includes information about some of his or her books, the purpose of the piece is to tell about the author's style. The book summaries provide evidence supporting the student writer's opinion about the author.

Practice/Apply

Have students identify the writer's opinion about the author and details from each book that support this point of view.

Minilesson 136

Organizing Details

Common Core State Standard: W.6.1.a

Objective: Clearly organize details.

Guiding Question: How should I arrange details?

Teach/Model

Remind students that in any writing, details must be in a logical order. Explain that in the author response, the student writer first summarized one book, then summarized the second book, then connected both books to his opinion about the author's style.

Practice/Apply

Have students choose two books by the same author and write an opinion statement about the author. Then, have them fill out an outline, idea-support map, or other graphic organizer with details that support their opinion about the author.

Book Review

Book Review

A **book review** is an essay that analyzes a book and gives the writer's opinion of it.

Parts of a Book Review

- The writer's thoughts, feelings, and ideas about the book
- An analysis of the book's characters, plot, and setting
- Details and examples from the book that support the writer's opinion

Introduction
Tells what the book is about in two sentences

A topic sentence states the writer's opinion and main idea.

Body
Tells the plot and the writer's opinion

These paragraphs summarize the plot and how the main characters interact.

Johnny Tremain by Esther Forbes

Johnny Tremain is the story of a teen boy whose life changes in unexpected ways. What makes this common subject different is that the book's setting is Boston at the time of the American Revolution. The historical setting and characters bring *Johnny Tremain* to life in interesting ways.

The story begins in 1773. Johnny, a 14-year-old orphan, works for Ephraim Lapham, a silversmith. Johnny is a skilled artist in silver, and he knows it. He brags about his talent and behaves rudely to Mr. Lapham's other workers. Then, Johnny burns his hand in a puddle of hot silver. Since he is no longer useful to the Laphams, he loses his job.

Things go from bad to worse for Johnny. He cannot find a job to make a living, and he does not have a home. Then Johnny meets Rab Silsbee. Rab is a member of the Sons of Liberty, a group of patriots who are protesting against British rule and taxes. Through Rab, Johnny meets historical figures like Samuel Adams and John Hancock. He becomes part of the events that lead to the American Revolution, such as the Boston Tea Party and Paul Revere's ride. The book ends with Johnny joining the Patriot Army.

Details about plot, character, and setting support the writer's opinion.

Conclusion
Restates the main idea and the writer's opinion

Esther Forbes presents Johnny's world so realistically that sometimes it's hard to tell which characters and events are real and which are made up. She describes Boston as a city of cobblestone streets, lively sailors, and milkmaids driving cows to the Boston Common (which today still exists as a park). Readers meet imaginary characters like Lydia, an African servant who is secretly a Patriot spy, as well as real people from that time period.

Johnny Tremain is an exciting book with many plot twists. The novel also shows how history changes people. Esther Forbes wrote the book during World War II, when lots of young Americans found their lives suddenly changed by history. For that reason, the book had meaning for readers back then. History is happening around us, too, so Johnny's story has meaning for readers today. That is why I would recommend *Johnny Tremain*.

Note how the author of this piece

- Organized the book review in a logical way, describing the plot in time order and then giving his opinions.
- Gave a positive opinion of the book.
  Another way he could have reviewed the book is to suggest changes to the book.

  Although I enjoyed reading *Johnny Tremain*, some readers might be confused if they have not yet learned about the American Revolution. The author should have included more background information.

WRITING MODELS AND FORMS

Minilesson 137

Introducing the Book Review

Common Core State Standard: W.6.4

Objective: Use the pages to recognize the parts of a book review.

Guiding Question: What should I tell about a book I have read?

Teach/Model

Have students read pp. 150–151. Point out that the beginning summarizes the plot in two sentences. Then the next few paragraphs retell a few of the main events in the order in which they happened in the book.

Practice/Apply

Have students identify clues in the model that show the sequence of events (examples: *begins, then, since, ends*).

Minilesson 138

Writing a Review vs. a Summary

Common Core State Standard: W.6.4

Objective: Recognize differences between a summary and a book review.

Guiding Question: How do reviews and summaries differ?

Teach/Model

Remind students that to summarize is to restate important ideas in their own words. A book review includes a summary of the book, as well as the writer's analysis of the book's characters, plot, and setting.

Practice/Apply

Have students locate paragraphs summarizing the book and identify the writer's opinions and analysis of the book. Together, write a paragraph reviewing a book you have read.

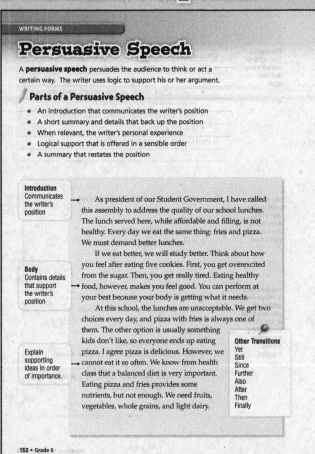

Persuasive Speech

Persuasive Speech

A **persuasive speech** persuades the audience to think or act a certain way. The writer uses logic to support his or her argument.

Parts of a Persuasive Speech

- An introduction that communicates the writer's position
- A short summary and details that back up the position
- When relevant, the writer's personal experience
- Logical support that is offered in a sensible order
- A summary that restates the position

Introduction
Communicates the writer's position

As president of our Student Government, I have called this assembly to address the quality of our school lunches. The lunch served here, while affordable and filling, is not healthy. Every day we eat the same thing: fries and pizza. We must demand better lunches.

Body
Contains details that support the writer's position

If we eat better, we will study better. Think about how you feel after eating five cookies. First, you get overexcited from the sugar. Then, you get really tired. Eating healthy food, however, makes you feel good. You can perform at your best because your body is getting what it needs.

At this school, the lunches are unacceptable. We get two choices every day, and pizza with fries is always one of them. The other option is usually something kids don't like, so everyone ends up eating pizza. I agree pizza is delicious. However, we cannot eat it so often. We know from health class that a balanced diet is very important. Eating pizza and fries provides some nutrients, but not enough. We need fruits, vegetables, whole grains, and light dairy.

Explain supporting ideas in order of importance.

Other Transitions
Yet
Still
Since
Further
Also
After
Then
Finally

When relevant, share your personal experience.

Here is what I imagine: a stocked salad bar with many choices. A salad bar is a good idea because it offers a lot of healthy options. Students will be able to pick exactly what they want. If a student does not like eggs, for example, he or she can skip the eggs and eat other things.

I had a meeting with Principal Ross to talk about all of this. I learned that we do not have healthy food because it is expensive. Principal Ross told me that it is cheaper to serve frozen fries than fresh fruits and vegetables. I know money is a big deal, but I believe health is even more important. So we students must demand better food.

Later today, I will pass around a petition saying we need healthy food options during lunch. Specifically, it suggests a salad bar and freshly cooked meals. When you see the petition, please sign it. Our bodies are important, and our bodies prefer fresh food. So stand up for your health and sign the petition. Demand a salad bar. Demand fresh meals. Demand something other than daily pizza and fries!

Ending
Contains a call to action, or words telling the audience what to do

Note how the author of this speech

- Uses *imperative* language—language that tells the audience what we should or must do.
- Other ways the author could have been persuasive are to ask questions or offer statistics.

How do you feel after eating fries? Would you rather eat greasy fries or a crisp pear?

Eight out of ten fifth-graders are tired of our school lunches.

WRITING MODELS AND FORMS

Minilesson 139

Introducing the Persuasive Speech

Common Core State Standards: W.6.1a, W.6.1b

Objective: Use the pages to learn what to include in a persuasive speech.

Guiding Question: How do I write a speech that convinces the audience to agree with my ideas?

Teach/Model

Have students read pp. 152–153. Add that the student writer included strong words, such as *demand* and *unacceptable*. Explain that these words are persuasive and encourage readers to agree with the writer's opinion.

Practice/Apply

Have students identify in the model the parts of a persuasive speech explained in the bulleted list.

Minilesson 140

Connecting with an Audience

Common Core State Standard: W.6.1b

Objective: Include details to connect with an audience.

Guiding Question: How can I connect with my audience?

Teach/Model

In order to persuade the audience, the student writer anticipated and addressed their thoughts (ex: *I agree pizza is delicious*); then showed why his goal is more important (*we cannot eat it so often*). He also used words and phrases to connect the audience to his goal (*We know from health class…*).

Practice/Apply

Have students identify examples of how the writer addressed possible concerns of the audience. Ask them to suggest other details the writer could add to connect with the audience.

Notetaking Strategies

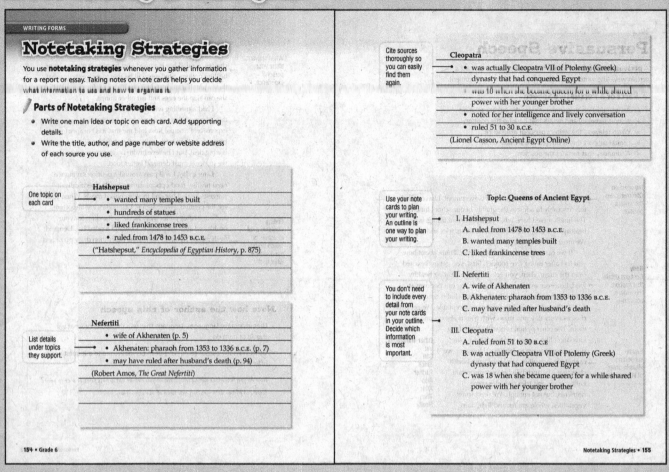

Notetaking Strategies

You use **notetaking strategies** whenever you gather information for a report or essay. Taking notes on note cards helps you decide what information to use and how to organize it.

Parts of Notetaking Strategies

- Write one main idea or topic on each card. Add supporting details.
- Write the title, author, and page number or website address of each source you use.

One topic on each card

Hatshepsut
- wanted many temples built
- hundreds of statues
- liked frankincense trees
- ruled from 1478 to 1453 B.C.E.

("Hatshepsut," *Encyclopedia of Egyptian History*, p. 875)

List details under topics they support.

Nefertiti
- wife of Akhenaten (p. 5)
- Akhenaten: pharaoh from 1353 to 1336 B.C.E. (p. 7)
- may have ruled after husband's death (p. 94)

(Robert Amos, *The Great Nefertiti*)

Cite sources thoroughly so you can easily find them again.

Cleopatra
- was actually Cleopatra VII of Ptolemy (Greek) dynasty that had conquered Egypt
- was 18 when she became queen; for a while shared power with her younger brother
- noted for her intelligence and lively conversation
- ruled 51 to 30 B.C.E.

(Lionel Casson, Ancient Egypt Online)

Use your note cards to plan your writing. An outline is one way to plan your writing.

Topic: Queens of Ancient Egypt

I. Hatshepsut
   A. ruled from 1478 to 1453 B.C.E.
   B. wanted many temples built
   C. liked frankincense trees

You don't need to include every detail from your note cards in your outline. Decide which information is most important.

II. Nefertiti
   A. wife of Akhenaten
   B. Akhenaten: pharaoh from 1353 to 1336 B.C.E.
   C. may have ruled after husband's death

III. Cleopatra
   A. ruled from 51 to 30 B.C.E
   B. was actually Cleopatra VII of Ptolemy (Greek) dynasty that had conquered Egypt
   C. was 18 when she became queen; for a while shared power with her younger brother

---

WRITING MODELS AND FORMS

Minilesson 141

Introducing Notetaking Strategies

Common Core State Standard: W.6.8

Objective: Recognize strategies for recording information.

Guiding Question: How can I record facts I have found?

Teach/Model

Read pp. 154–155 aloud. Add that notes do not have to be complete sentences and that the page number is at the bottom of the first note card since each fact was on the same page of the book. Page numbers are included after each fact on the second note card since the facts were found on different pages.

Practice/Apply

Have students discuss the details about each source included on the note cards.

Minilesson 142

Writing an Outline

Common Core State Standard: W.6.8

Objective: Organize research to create an outline.

Guiding Question: How do I create an outline?

Teach/Model

Tell students that after completing research, writers organize the information in a way that makes sense. An outline is one way to do this. Explain that the topic is at the top, the main points are listed beside the Roman numerals, and supporting details are written below each Roman numeral.

Practice/Apply

Have pairs create an outline using their own research notes or notes that you provide to them. Remind them to arrange main ideas and supporting details in a logical order.

Journal

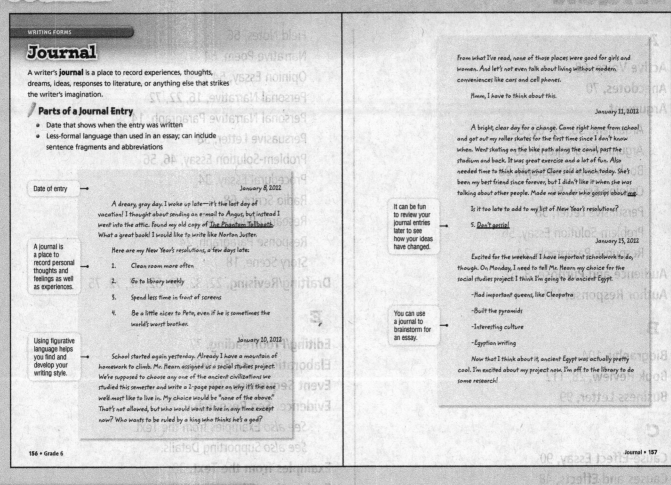

WRITING FORMS
Journal

A writer's **journal** is a place to record experiences, thoughts, dreams, ideas, responses to literature, or anything else that strikes the writer's imagination.

Parts of a Journal Entry
- Date that shows when the entry was written
- Less-formal language than used in an essay; can include sentence fragments and abbreviations

Date of entry →

January 8, 2012

A dreary, gray day. I woke up late—it's the last day of vacation! I thought about sending an e-mail to Angus, but instead I went into the attic. Found my old copy of *The Phantom Tollbooth*. What a great book! I would like to write like Norton Juster.

Here are my New Year's resolutions, a few days late:

1. Clean room more often
2. Go to library weekly
3. Spend less time in front of screens
4. Be a little nicer to Pete, even if he is sometimes the world's worst brother.

A journal is a place to record personal thoughts and feelings as well as experiences.

January 10, 2012

School started again yesterday. Already I have a mountain of homework to climb. Mr. Hearn assigned us a social studies project. We're supposed to choose any one of the ancient civilizations we studied this semester and write a 2-page paper on why it's the one we'd most like to live in. My choice would be "none of the above." That's not allowed, but who would want to live in any time except now? Who wants to be ruled by a king who thinks he's a god?

Using figurative language helps you find and develop your writing style.

156 • Grade 6

From what I've read, none of those places were good for girls and women. And let's not even talk about living without modern conveniences like cars and cell phones.

Hmm, I have to think about this.

January 11, 2012

A bright, clear day for a change. Came right home from school and got out my roller skates for the first time since I don't know when. Went skating on the bike path along the canal, past the stadium and back. It was great exercise and a lot of fun. Also needed time to think about what Clare said at lunch today. She's been my best friend since forever, but I didn't like it when she was talking about other people. Made me wonder who gossips about *me*.

Is it too late to add to my list of New Year's resolutions?

5. *Don't gossip!*

It can be fun to review your journal entries later to see how your ideas have changed.

January 13, 2012

Excited for the weekend! I have important schoolwork to do, though. On Monday, I need to tell Mr. Hearn my choice for the social studies project. I think I'm going to do ancient Egypt.

-Had important queens, like Cleopatra

-Built the pyramids

-Interesting culture

-Egyptian writing

You can use a journal to brainstorm for an essay.

Now that I think about it, ancient Egypt was actually pretty cool. I'm excited about my project now. I'm off to the library to do some research!

Journal • 157

WRITING MODELS AND FORMS

Minilesson 143

Introducing the Journal

Common Core State Standard: W.6.10

Objective: Understand how to write a journal.

Guiding Question: What do I write in my journal?

Teach/Model

Have students read pp. 156–157. Explain that writers can record anything in a journal, and point out that each sample entry includes a different type of information. Point out the dates, and explain that the student writer included entries for most days but did not write every day.

Practice/Apply

Have students discuss the type of information recorded in each entry (ex: *personal thoughts, outline for schoolwork*). Have them discuss how the writer's journal might help her write other projects.

Minilesson 144

Writing for Oneself

Common Core State Standard: W.6.10

Objective: Recognize differences between formal and personal writing.

Guiding Question: How do I write for myself?

Teach/Model

Remind students that writing varies depending on the audience and purpose. A journal is personal, so the audience includes only the writer. Point out that the sample journal is written using informal language and includes incomplete sentences, abbreviations, and initials.

Practice/Apply

Have students underline and explain examples of how the journal entry is different from formal writing, such as a school assignment.

Writing for Common Core • 115

Index